a STRING of
Hope

a STRING of Hope

Inspiration from Korea

MIN GYOO SHIN

BEACON HILL PRESS
OF KANSAS CITY

Beacon Hill Press of Kansas City
PO Box 419527
Kansas City, MO 64141
beaconhillbooks.com

978-0-8341-3649-6

Printed in the
United States of America

Cover Design: Mike Williams
Interior Design: Sharon Page

Library of Congress Cataloging-in-Publication Data
Names: Sin, Min-gyu, 1958- author.
Title: A string of hope / Min Gyoo Shin.
Description: Kansas City, MO : Beacon Hill Press of Kansas City, [2017]
Identifiers: LCCN 2017001392 | ISBN 9780834136496 (pbk.)
Subjects: LCSH: Sangam-dong Kyohoe (Seoul, Korea)--History. | Pastoral theology. | Church. |
  Seoul (Korea)--Church history.
Classification: LCC BX8699.N37 S46 2017 | DDC 287.9/9095195--dc23 LC record available at
https://lccn.loc.gov/2017001392

10 9 8 7 6 5 4 3 2 1

⊕ CONTENTS

Preface   7

1. Give All You've Got in Every Situation   9
2. Harmony for Church Growth   12
3. Priority   14
4. From Laziness to Patience: The Key Is Prayer   17
5. Overcome Challenges through Dawn Prayer Worship   20
6. Harmony between New and Old Members   23
7. Keep the Companionship   25
8. Weak but Valuable   27
9. Kingdom Citizens   29
10. Look Far Ahead   32
11. Before Blaming Others   34
12. First Love   37
13. Love Others as They Need   39
14. This Too Shall Pass   41
15. Forgive First   43
16. Depression, Friends, and Firm Relationships   45
17. The Language of Christians   48
18. The Best Gift   50
19. Honest before God   53
20. The Church's Responsibility for Its Children   56
21. Beautiful Sacrifice of Couples   58
22. The Holy Spirit's Church   61
23. Happiness Is Near   64
24. A Noisy Church Is a Servant Church   67

25. Ministry to the Elderly: Silver School   70
26. Expression of Care through Practical Sacrifice   72
27. Righteous Ministry Decisions   74
28. We Are God's Masterpieces   77
29. Disability Ministry: SNTC   79
30. When You Give, Give All   83
31. Church Is a Sanctuary with Kindness and Trust   86
32. Giving Immediate Help   89
33. Helping to Solve Heart Issues   92
34. Passion: Crisis Turns into Opportunity   95
35. The Most Precious Being   98
36. Give Thanks with the Heart of a Debtor   101
37. Effective Ministry   103
38. A Vision for Remote Areas   106
39. Rebuild the Collapsed Temple   109
40. Recalling the Days   111
41. A Church Raising up Another Church   113
42. The Budget: Never to Be Grudged or Spared   116
43. Being One with People   118
44. A Sending Church   120
45. Overcoming Limitations   122
46. Sponsoring Seminarians   124
47. Wishes for the Future Pastor   126
48. Dreaming for One More Righteous Man   129
49. My Wish for Korean Churches   132
50. My Wish for Korean Churches (Part Two)   134
Epilogue   136

⊕ PREFACE

Few people know the true meaning of the word *hope*. It appears that we only know the meaning of this word in casual society, but it does not have an application to our lives. *Have hope, We have a hope, Do not lose your hope,* and other examples have become conventional words of encouragement and abstract advice that does not provide much inspiration or meaning.

This inclination exists in the church as well. Preachers and believers in fellowship place an emphasis on hope, but it becomes too obvious and meaningless. This is a very sad situation.

Hope may be a hopeless word. Hope is certainly not an easy word. But we must clearly remember one thing. For Christians, the true meaning of hope resides in other worlds. We cannot fully appreciate the meaning of hope in *this* world. For the children of God, hope contains more meanings beyond the obvious. The hope we Christians have comes from the almighty God. Situations or conditions are irrelevant. Human understanding and human ability do not make any sense in front of God. The hope is with us when we are standing with the God who loves us most.

My church and I experienced a miraculous hope. God has led us much more than we could have imagined through innumerable hopeless situations. When I look back, I still can't believe the many evidences that stood in opposition to our hope. Yet I am convinced that these stories of miraculous hope do not happen only in my church.

This book describes how God has led Sangamdong Church of the Nazarene and how God wants us to go beyond our limitations. I want to share these stories both with my congregation and with the rest of the world. Yet I do not seek to boost myself. Furthermore, our church stories are not a source of pride. It is all about the story of our Father. We are just means of his work. This is the story of hope that God wants to tell you. With this story, my church and I are challenged to see the hope and go beyond our comfort zone, and I hope you will be challenged in the same way.

A string of hope is one. The string we each hold is not different. Someone does not hold a strong and thick string while others cling to a thin one. The string from God is the same, and we each hold it. Let us hold to this hope until the end, regardless of any circumstances. Our God will never forget us or leave us alone.

I pray this book can be its own string of hope for churches enduring a depression, a slump, or seemingly endless struggles. I pray that we all find the *String of Hope* coming from our Father. I also pray to hear stories from other churches who have experienced even greater miracles from the hope of God.

I look forward to seeing all of God's children praise the Lord with the song of hope.

—Rev. Min Gyoo Shin

1 ⊕ GIVE ALL YOU'VE GOT IN EVERY SITUATION

The inscription on Ruby Kendrick's tombstone reads, "If I had a thousand lives to give Korea should have them all." Ruby came to Korea as a young missionary but passed away from a disease on June 19, 1908, at the age of twenty-six—after just eight months in language school. Yet her death was not in vain because it led a number of young missionaries to come to Korea to follow her example. They brought the gospel to this land and led its people to Jesus Christ.

Another story of a young but impactful death is found in Anne Frank's life—introduced through her book *The Diary of Anne Frank*. Others include Joongseob Lee, a brilliant Korean artist who passed away at the age of forty; Bruce Lee, a well-known actor from Hong Kong who died at the age of thirty-three; and Sowol Kim, a famous Korean poet known for his work "Azalea," who died at the age of thirty-two. There are many other examples of young but impactful deaths in this world, and Jesus Christ is chief among them, only thirty-three when he died on the cross. In spite of their short time on this earth, the lives of these people yielded abundant fruit—evidenced by the influence they have had on the people of our time.

You may know of other examples of lives that were short but fruitful. None of us knows how long our life on this earth will be, but one thing we need to remember is that our lives have great eternal value. With that in mind, we need to focus on giving our best and using all our strength in every situation in which we find ourselves.

If we value our lives, it is essential for us to eat well to keep in good health. More importantly, we need to give everything we have, using all of our strength and abilities in the positions we are in. Doing so adds even greater value to our lives.

In my early years of ministry, shortly after dawn, I routinely went to the church to have a time of worship in prayer until it was time for work. Although it only took about five minutes to get home, I chose to stay at the church instead of going home to rest for two reasons. First, with my wife teaching at Korea Nazarene University (KNU) in Cheonan City and my son studying in a province, I did not have anyone to welcome me home, and I did not have any desire to go into a cold house that was empty most of the time.

Second, I told myself, "I would rather rest or take a nap in the church!" So I always came back to my office after the early-morning prayer and worship time. There, I could continue my prayer time, or sometimes I dozed off. My breakfast was a simple cereal or grain drink that I prepared myself. Then my day started and typically lasted until late at night, focusing on the ministry in the church.

Some might take pity on me to hear about those days and the situation I found myself in. Indeed, how miserable it was to arrive home after a tough day just to find out I was alone with no one to welcome me home! Pastoral ministry is a wonderful gift from God, yet I know family life is also a great gift from him. After I quit my job teaching at KNU and came to pastor the church, I was not able to enjoy my family life for a time. Although it was lonely, I did not let myself get discouraged. I discovered I could find advantages in the situation I was in. Having spare time as a functionally "single" man, I began to focus more on ministry. This period of time was God's gift for me when I was just beginning my pastoral career.

I believed that the position assigned to me was directed by God. I knew he would never leave me in a place where I was not supposed to be and that he would take me out of it if he wanted. So I was standing where God had set me. The conditions seemed difficult, but it was just what God had prepared for me.

What is left, then, but to give it all you've got in every situation? No conditions, no *ifs*. We need to control each situation we find ourselves in and not be controlled by it. If we give everything we have in every situation, we will be properly utilizing the gifts God has given us. It is not a matter of how many years we have left on this earth. Rather, in every role we have, we ought to put all of our strength into building up our family, our church, and our community. If we do everything we can, using every bit of strength we have—even if the fruit of our efforts appears after we have passed away—rest assured, we *will* receive our crown from God.

2 ⊕ HARMONY FOR CHURCH GROWTH

In his book *Pensées* Blaise Pascal, a French Christian philosopher, wrote that human beings need to harmonize with three subjects. Pascal explains that we can never be happy if any of these relationships gets broken or becomes problematic.

The first subject for people to harmonize with is themselves. Those who do not understand what they want and are dishonest or deceitful to themselves cannot be happy. Next is harmony with our neighbors. Happiness will be impossible if we fail to build harmonious relationships with our neighbors. When we know how to cooperate with others, we get to share mutual help and the joy of relational growth. Lastly, Pascal emphasizes that harmonizing with God is even more important than the other two. Yet our sin hinders us from obtaining harmony with God. And the problem of sin cannot be solved without Jesus Christ.

When Pascal talked about growth, and when we talk about church growth, we are not referring only to external growth but also inner, spiritual growth. This principle of harmony is critical to growing the church.

Sangamdong Church of the Nazarene listed four criteria for its pastors to meet in order to ensure harmony and growth in the church. Most of these values are equally important for both pastors and laypeople and should be implemented in everyone's lives.

First, many hours should be spent reading the Bible and in prayer. These hours will never be spent in vain but will help you reach your goals. Also, for pastors specifically, never neglect or put off preparing your sermons.

Second, set high expectations for your church and its members. Setting high expectations includes being sensitive to the needs of your church members while also firmly encouraging them with biblical teaching. We would say bring the Bible in one hand and the newspaper in the other.

Third, evangelism must be a priority. Nowadays, a lot of people in Korean churches say that evangelism is not "working" anymore. However, I believe the kingdom of God will surely be expanded if we evangelize with perseverance and long-term vision.

Fourth, do not be absent from your office. Pastors need to set a good example of arriving at the office on time and being there during the workday—physically separating the parsonage from the office.

I humbly share these statements with my mentees when they ask me for advice. There may be other obligations that individual pastors must focus on, yet these four points should not be overlooked. If these four criteria became the philosophy of every pastor, then their congregants would be influenced to live God-centered lives themselves.

When applying these four statements to laypeople, the first and third statements would be applicable as stated, but the other two would need to be reworded. The second point can be reworded to state, "Set high expectations for your church to meet the needs and expectations of nonbelievers." If the pastor builds up the church with high expectations for church members and then those members, along with the pastor, set high expectations for themselves to meet the expectations of nonbelievers, the church will have no choice but to grow. The fourth point also may be restated for an individual as, "Give all of your strength in your church, in your home, and in your workplace." We bring glory to God when we give our all to everything we do, and we influence nonbelievers in a good way as they see Christians exemplify what it is to be a good citizen. These tenets are the very basis of church growth.

3 ⊕ PRIORITY

In Sangamdong, there are a number of beautiful parks: Park of Peace, Nanji Han River Park, Nanjicheon Park, Sky Park, and Sunset Park are among them. In the early mornings, you will see a lot of people walking, jogging, riding bikes, and playing badminton. They work hard to stay healthy. The Bible says our body is where the Spirit dwells, so we need to regard it as valuable. First Timothy 4:8 says, "For physical training is of some value . . ." And yet, if keeping physically healthy occupied all of our time and was what we continually thought about, that would be problematic. For instance, if we were tempted to miss a worship service or church fellowship gathering in order to go play golf with friends, that mentality could lead to trouble. Or if you travel great distances just to visit a restaurant known for a healthy dish, this could be a problem as well. The desire, whether conscious or unconscious, to be perfectly healthy has the potential of becoming an idol. Staying healthy is important, but that cannot be our main purpose. Training our bodies to work for and serve the Lord will be of more value than health-driven training.

I remember a young Korean celebrity whose reputation was harmed by scandalous allegations of squandering money and gambling abroad. Pleasure is a blessing from God, but when pleasure becomes the purpose of our lives, it becomes an idol. The apostle Paul condemned those who found pleasure in eating to extremes by asserting that "their god is their stomach" (Philippians 3:19). Having good food is a great pleasure, but if we so long to fill our stomach that our longing changes our life's priority, we have an issue.

All kinds of addiction are related to pleasure. Why do people become alcoholic? Isn't it because of alcohol's nature of bringing pleasure to us? Nowadays a lot of people stay up late or even all night in front of the computer, indulging in online gambling or pornography or any number of vices available on the internet. They even regularly visit an internet cafe if they don't have that availability at home. Addiction to the internet's vices is a serious problem, especially with children. I still remember when a lot of fans of the famous golfer Tiger Woods were disappointed to hear the news of his sexual scandal, which left him disgraced and his lovely family broken.

Sports activities, hobbies, and relaxing are fine if they are not excessive. We should limit the activities in which we find pleasure in order to protect our Christian faith.

Then what is to be prioritized in our lives? Worship. We have three sessions of worship at Sangamdong Church on Sundays. An early-morning worship service is led by the assistant pastors in turn. I lead the second and third sessions. The second service is more traditional in its style, and the third is rather contemporary. Attenders are allowed to choose the style of worship they prefer most, but attenders usually choose based on service times rather than preferred worship styles because of their busy schedules. It would be difficult to change this tendency in people, so my back-up plan to solve this problem is cell groups. By mobilizing small groups in the church, I encourage them to recover the essence of worship and learn to prioritize it in their lives. Without changing the worship service at the surface level, I hope that genuine worship is found and practiced in the small groups.

One of the good things we experience in the small groups is that we can share the Word of God with deeper impact. As we recover the essence of true worship and learn to prioritize it in small groups, it will spill over into the church's corporate worship services. We eventually will choose to attend a certain worship service because we love to worship rather than because it is scheduled at a convenient time. When we choose to worship intentionally rather than because of a schedule, we can better concentrate on worshiping and communing with our Lord. We have hope at Sangamdong Church that we will one day be a congregation full of people who make worship a priority above everything else in their lives.

4 ⊕ FROM LAZINESS TO PATIENCE: THE KEY IS PRAYER

A crab was dying, drying out on a high rock beside the surf. The crab had enough energy to go back to the sea, but he didn't have the wisdom to take action. Without making any effort to reach the surf just one meter away, which would bring him back to the sea, he just waited for the wave to reach him. It was obvious that soon he would dry up and die.

In our lives, we sometimes meet a surf that carries us into a spot with a hurdle. Like the surf that set the crab on the rock and never returned to bring him back, so there will come situations in our lives that drive us into a corner. If we lie down where we are and wait for another big wave to come and save our lives, we may be stuck there forever. Proverbs 19:15 says, "Laziness brings on deep sleep, and the shiftless go hungry." Sometimes, though, patience can be mistaken for laziness. Laziness is doing nothing and expecting nothing. Meanwhile, patience is responsible for the given task with a fervent hope for success.

The word *patience* has its root in the Latin *pati*, which is a combination of the words *passive* and *passion*. When churches are newly planted or very small, pastors may easily drift between laziness and patience. Pastors need to wait patiently for the coming fruit, yet they can't sit around and do nothing, nor should they toil without a purpose.

When I first stepped foot in Sangamdong Church, they were renting the second and third floors of someone else's building. The actual space was under 198 square meters. The second floor housed a pastoral office and an open area for Sunday school classes as well as a dining area with a small kitchen. And on the third floor there was a traditional sanctuary with long, wooden benches and a podium. I remember about sixty people attended the worship service on my first Sunday as the pastor. One woman and four men sang in the choir.

I had to lead a dawn prayer service every morning. While I taught at KNU, I didn't take the time to attend dawn prayer worship at church. And when I was a student at KNU, I was often absent from drawn prayer worship. I remember Chang sool Gong, the president of KNU, knocking on the door to the dormitory early every morning, inviting students to the morning prayer worship. I used to respond, "Have a safe trip, sir!" without even opening my eyes. I didn't want to sacrifice my sweet sleep back then. When I studied in the U.S., I attended dawn prayer services out of obligation, not out of the desire of my heart. I have to confess that I didn't know the true joy of dawn prayer back then.

Now I was the senior pastor of Sangamdong Church, and I had to lead dawn prayer worship every morning. The first morning, however, only one elderly woman appeared at the service. And the next morning and the next and the next, it continued to be only Jongsoon Chung who attended the dawn prayer worship. Then I felt a conflict between my laziness and my patience. I had to do my best to revive the dawn prayer services, yet I had to wait with patience. The thing that is needed most in this kind of situation is prayer. I was reminded of a saying during my Bible college days: "Without prayer, there will be no church revival!"

One day, I asked Mrs. Chung to bring me a photo of her family. I promised her that I would pray for each member of her family every morning. I kept the photo in my prayer notebook and never forgot to pray for them. When I prayed with her every morning, I named out loud each member of her family with a sincere heart. This practice of mine gradually became known among the rest of the church members, and one by one, others started to join our dawn prayer worship. I asked each of them to bring me a family photo, and so the number of photos in my prayer notebook grew.

Prayer can resolve the conflict between laziness and patience. We need to wait patiently but not be lazy. It is possible with patience through prayer. Waiting while praying may feel like you are doing nothing, but don't be deceived. Prayer teaches patience. It should be the most important tool for church planters. It has the power to move the spirit of people as well as the Spirit of God.

5 ⊕ OVERCOME CHALLENGES THROUGH DAWN PRAYER WORSHIP

There once was a rich man who purchased a beautiful island. He planted trees and flowers and eventually covered the island with green pastures. He raised rabbits and deer in this wonderful garden of his. At one point, he found that the animals were getting weaker and their fur and eyes had lost their brightness. He thought, *How can they be sick in these perfect conditions?* So he found a wise man in a village.

The wise man advised the rich man to bring a wolf to the island. Seeing his astonishment, the wise man explained, "Their sickness is coming from the perfect environment. If they have to run fast to get away from the wolf in order to survive, you will see that their fur and eyes will soon be refreshed."

To the rich man's surprise, the animals soon recovered their strength once the wolf had been set among them.

This story applies to humans and especially Christians in the same way. When we are not challenged in life, we can lose our focus and soon become complacent. Thankfully, most of us do continue to face challenges in our lives. Thus, our lives then depend on how we respond to these challenges. We should not avoid reality or give up hope, just as birds need to flap their wings against the flow of air and fish cannot live without water even though they must swim against it.

King David became a hero because of Goliath. Hannah, the mother of the prophet Samuel, became a woman of prayer as a result of provocation from her rival, Peninnah. Windsurfers wait for strong winds, as do those wanting to fly kites. And flowers that bloom after experiencing a severe winter are known for their great beauty. We cannot stand still when facing a crisis. If the rich man who owned the island had not taken the advice of the wise man, his rabbits and deer would have eventually died off.

Sangamdong Church also experienced a number of difficult situations while it was still a small congregation in rented space. I couldn't just stand there and watch the crisis. There is a saying that "every crisis is an opportunity." I used the Sangamdong Church's crisis as a turning point for a new start. The thing I chose to focus on and resolve was the dawn prayer.

As I shared earlier, I was lazy about attending dawn prayer worship as a Bible college student, so it was not easy to prepare for leading it as a pastor. I not only needed to attend, but I also needed to prepare a devotional for each service. Through this time, I learned the secret for bringing new life to a church and its people, and that secret is prayer. I am a witness to the stability and health of the families who are committed to the dawn prayer service. I knew that principle would be the same for myself, so I have made dawn prayer worship a priority in my life and pastoral ministry.

Since I had dual responsibilities as the senior pastor of Sangamdong Church and the president of Korea Nazarene University, my schedule was tight. One might think that continuing the commitment to the dawn prayer service would be too difficult. However, I led the service every morning and then took the express train to Cheonan City, where KNU is located.

I regarded my position at KNU as a ministry, although a university position is more of a job that can take double the energy for the same amount of work, and there is a high level of stress associated with it. As you can imagine, most of the reports given in a university president's office are not enjoyable. Because of this, it was easy to get down spiritually. After a day of work at KNU, I traveled back to the church by train, and there I prepared for the next day's dawn prayer service. There were days that I fell fast asleep as I prepared the devotional messages. Sometimes there were only a few short hours before time to lead the next service. But I am amazed at how, because of the dawn prayer service, God refreshed my spirit and gave me the strength I needed to sustain me for the rest of that day. My batteries were drained and almost dead after a day of work at KNU, only to be recharged through dawn prayer worship the next morning.

I realized through this time that worshiping God through the dawn prayer service gives life to us. It gives life to the church members but also to me. I need to be revived myself before I can revive my people. If the pastor slacks off, the whole church will slack off too. That is the reason the pastor needs to focus on keeping his grip tight on the commitment.

When I am traveling and miss several days of dawn prayer worship, my body gets used to the new schedule amazingly fast. I have to push myself and discipline my body to remain faithful to my rhythm of life with dawn prayer worship. I think God shows his compassion for my efforts because he has never failed to sustain me as I lead the prayer worship time.

As a pastor, I have always emphasized the importance of dawn prayer worship. After years of my emphasis, the attenders gradually increased—especially during the forty days of specific worship when we had three hundred in attendance. About nine hundred adults regularly attend Sunday morning worship services at Sangamdong Church. Our attendance at the dawn prayer service continues to fluctuate, especially when I am traveling and cannot be there to lead it, but I am thankful that this type of worship has been revived. We will continue to emphasize this worship service and make every effort to increase attendance over the long term because I believe that the practice of dawn prayer worship has the potential to bring revival to each member, to the church, and to our whole nation.

6 ⊕ HARMONY BETWEEN NEW AND OLD MEMBERS

There once was a man who bent down to pull weeds from his garden. As he pulled the weeds, beads of sweat fell from his face. He huffed and puffed and said, "This garden would be much nicer without these annoying weeds. Why did God create such a useless plant?"

Then a weed in the corner of that garden turned and spoke to him. "You think we are annoying and useless, but we are actually helping you! We lay down our roots deep into the soil and crush it, which prevents the soil from being washed away. During the dry season, we help keep the soil from being blown away. If we were not here in your garden, your plants would not grow because the rain would wash away the soil, and the wind would blow it away. You should give us thanks whenever you appreciate the beautiful flowers and plants in your garden."

It all depends on how you look at things. You can complain or be thankful. We can choose to be impressed by something, or we can overlook the very same thing.

Long before I came to Sangamdong Church, they had formed several small groups. By the grace of God, those small groups have grown to about twenty times their original size. This growth caused a new problem to surface: The old members and new members did not blend easily. As the senior pastor, I need to look at them from more than one point of view. As with the illustration of the weeds, I have learned that things that appear to be a problem can actually be necessary and beneficial if we look at the situation from a different point of view.

For example, the older members, with many years of service in the church and a keen understanding of the nature and structure of the church, have many strong opinions. This perspective can come across in a way that ostracizes the newer members, but that can be reversed if we look at the situation from a more positive point of view. Newer members ought to keep in mind that the strong opinions of the older members come from their deep love for and understanding of the history of the church. And, likewise, older members ought to realize that the new members are passionate about seeing the church thrive and continue long into the future. I admire the passion and love both sets of people have for the church.

In dealing with these issues, I decided not to look at either side from a negative perception, and I respected each of their hearts. I allowed the older members to be involved in the decision-making process for the major issues of the church, which gave them a feeling of respect. As a result, they served the church in even more sacrificial ways. In fact, they are the ones who have sustained the church over the long years. They deserved to be recognized for their sacrifices and contributions.

On the other hand, I gave the new members more opportunities to serve the church and its ministries. Of course, I encountered a number of difficulties during this process because some of the new members were satisfied with the new opportunities, but others complained about not having any major decision-making authority. I explained to them that my intent was to eventually include them in decision-making committees as they became more familiar with the vision and environment of the church.

My approach was effective in transforming both groups, and we were thankfully able to overcome our difficulties during this period of transition and church growth. A pastor should never show favoritism toward any church members nor look down on anyone with bias or prejudice but should, rather, treat all members with appropriately positive thoughts and actions. My dream is to be a pastor who understands and embraces all church members with that kind of attitude.

7 ⊕ KEEP THE COMPANIONSHIP

One day the tools in a carpenter's workshop gathered for a meeting. The hammer led the meeting as usual, but some of the other tools rebelled, complaining, "The hammer is always a breaker, crasher, and noise maker, so he needs to leave!"

The hammer replied, "All right, I admit my weakness, and I will agree to leave. But the smoothing plane needs to leave with me because he exposes the weaknesses of others rather than covering them."

The smoothing plane answered, "Okay, then the ruler should leave with us, because she always measures others as if she is the only correct person, and that hurts everyone."

The ruler pointed out, "The saw is not cooperating either. He always cuts and segregates us. So he is the most useless tool among us."

Then the saw shouted at the sandpaper, "You are too rough!"

In the middle of the chaos, the carpenter came into the shop and soon made a beautiful pulpit using all the tools. Each tool that had been pointing out others' weaknesses was astonished at the good work they had done when they were used together as a team. They realized that they were all the companions—or teammates—of the carpenter.

This analogy can apply to any organization, but it's especially appropriate in the church. We each have our own personalities and our own responsibilities. Our differences may cause conflict at times, but rather than disrespect one another, we should appreciate the differences and be thankful that others can do what we cannot do. We should not forget for a moment that we are a team.

Ordinary conflicts in a community tend to get worse when newcomers step in, just as we have often witnessed in Sangamdong Church. When I first arrived as the pastor at Sangamdong, I knew

I needed to be very careful. Not long after my first Sunday in the church, the annual meeting was held. Usually this is one of the biggest meetings in the church because every member is asked to attend. In my presentation, I expressed that I would pursue the plans the pastor who preceded me had set in place. Some of the church members disagreed with my idea and asked me to put forth a new plan of my own. I appreciated that they wanted to empower me as the new pastor, but I tried to persuade them otherwise. "I know the former pastor led this church for more than thirteen years, and I do not want to bulldoze those plans." I understood that not everyone agreed with my approach, but I felt that I needed to respect the former pastor and to work initially toward the goals he set before he left because I recognized that we were on the same team. When I think back on those days, I believe I made a good choice, and I believe the wisdom came from God.

Similar situations often happen in church contexts, and we need to understand the importance of companionship as a team. Instead of treating others who have different ideas as our enemies, we should think of them as teammates who seek our same goal or purpose. If there are problems, let God take care of them. What we need to do is to know when to respect others' opinions and when to be firm with our own.

This kind of companionship needs to be based on truthful respect for each other. Lay members and former pastors should also be respected. It is said that if a senior pastor serves a church for more than thirty years, it will take more than thirty additional years for the influence of his leadership to fade out of the church. For this reason, some churches ask their retiring senior pastors to attend other churches.

The way we deal with this issue in the church is vitally important. New pastors and existing church members should recognize the achievements of former senior pastors and never isolate them in the church. Their ministry should be recognized and appreciated. This philosophy has helped me maintain good relationships with former pastors.

8 ⊕ WEAK BUT VALUABLE

Have you ever felt weak and not very influential around others? We live in a competitive, high-stress society. Uncertain futures, extreme loneliness, and helpless isolation are part of all our lives. Our existence is not by our choice, and neither are our deaths. In the midst of this environment, we can easily become overwhelmed and be tempted to discredit ourselves. However, every individual is worthy of his or her existence. Being alive is powerful. Life itself has value. When we acknowledge the value of life itself, we acknowledge the value of being ourselves, and we see the value of others just as they are.

The purity of our hearts will show itself in our concern for others because being worthy involves being concerned. Showing concern for each member of the church does not just happen because of good intentions. We cannot pretend to be concerned for others merely to look good in order to increase membership. We are to show genuine concern because each individual is a valuable treasure!

When I was young, one of my older brothers told me a story that has since impacted my ministry. My brother served as a colonel at the army headquarters. As a colonel, he started his morning routine by making phone calls. His notebook contained lists of names to be called on a daily, weekly, bi-weekly, and monthly schedule. This routine helped him maintain positive relationships with others. Some might think it was just a ruse to earn social standing. But in reality, those efforts cannot be carried out only by pretense. I am sure the colonel knew the worthiness of the people around him, and he attempted to maintain healthy relationships with them, sacrificing his time to talk to them on the phone in the midst of his busy schedule.

Although I was just a young boy at the time, the strategy of this colonel impacted my life, and I was later able to apply this method in my ministry. When I started pastoring, our church was small, with only a few adults attending worship services. I began to call each of them every evening, knowing they would not refuse a phone call from the new pastor. And who can refuse someone's concern for them? I always remembered to ask how the elders were doing, and I also greeted the children with a small bag of treats as I stood at a crossroad in front of their school. And of course, I prayed for each of them, calling their individual names daily in my dawn prayer service.

Once again we see that, without recognizing the value of people, our concern will not be seen as genuine. What matters most to me is not the member of the church who gives the most or serves the most or who treats me well. *Everyone* is valuable to me. When we approach people with sincere hearts, their hearts will be open also!

I am worthy. I have value, and others also have value. A person, just by existing, is valuable. If we acknowledge this truth, we should express it to others. We are to treat others every day just as we would treat our most valuable treasures. Some may seem weak or feeble in our eyes, but in God's eyes, we are all valuable, and God adores us just as we are.

9 ⊕ KINGDOM CITIZENS

In the Roman Empire, the Roman citizens were afforded a number of privileges. They were given the right to vote, they were exempt from paying the ten-percent residential tax, and they were not subject to corporal punishment or torture until an official judgment from the court had been received. These privileges were given only to Roman citizens who were born citizens, who could afford to buy citizenship with a great amount of money, or who completed twenty-five years of service in the Roman military. After serving twenty-five years in the military, they were promoted to general and guaranteed a post-retirement pension. To survive twenty-five years of seemingly endless wars during that time period would have been quite a feat. However, people willingly gave their lives in this way in the hope of earning Roman citizenship.

In the middle of this very situation, Paul wrote to the members of the church at Philippi and said, "But our citizenship is in heaven" (3:20a). Considering that people were readily sacrificing their lives for national citizenship, no sacrifice could possibly be made to achieve the greater and more wonderful citizenship of the heavenly kingdom. What should we do with this marvelous kingdom citizenship that has been given to us? What kind of lives should we live to be worthy to be called kingdom citizens? First, since we have received the kingdom citizenship without cost, we must acknowledge that God is the Creator of the universe, and we must give our lives to the cause of his kingdom. Because we were freely given our kingdom citizenship, we have no attachment to this world, and nothing should be wasted or regretted.

By the grace of God, I was able to purchase a condo with the money I saved during the ten years I taught at Korea Nazarene University. I was so thankful to finally be able to provide a nest for my family. But when the time came to start constructing our church building, I felt compelled to give what I had to the Lord. I decided to give my condo to God because he is the owner. For two years, I also sacrificed my salary from the church as an offering for the new building. Then the church members began to do the same and give what they had to the church. A gratitude that far outweighed the joy of owning my own condo filled my heart in that experience. The voluntary sacrifices of pastors open new avenues for kingdom expansion.

While I was pastoring a church in the United States, I had an opportunity to have dinner with Robert Cerrato, who was the district superintendent of the Kansas District of the Church of the Nazarene at that time. In my country, it is customary to treat a person in a higher position to a meal, so I wanted to take Rev. Cerrato to a nice restaurant. After dinner, as I was about to pay the bill, he stopped me in order to pay it himself. I said to him, "I am treating you, so please be my guest this time."

But he insisted that the meal was on him, saying, "Who do you think has more money between you and me?"

This was a simple event, but I was shocked by the American perspective. He understood my pastoral situation of serving a church in a rented space. As a result, he felt it was reasonable for him—in a better financial position—to treat me to the meal. Through this experience, I realized how beautiful it is to share with each other in the kingdom of God. And it has inspired me to serve my own people in the same way. I have learned to serve the people not only with spiritual food but also with physical food in my practice as a kingdom citizen. When the love of God is shared, amazing things happen.

Once, I treated a church member to a bowl of noodle soup. It was just a simple meal, but he was impressed and said, "I grew up in a Christian family, but never in my life have I been treated by the pastor." His appreciation did not end there—I later found out he sold his house to give for the building project. I believe God will bless him greatly because he did not spare even his valuables in showing his gratitude to God. A small meal served in love moved the heart of a man, and God worked in the midst of that situation to urge him to give even bigger things to the Lord.

For what are we consuming what we have? Are we using our belongings to advance the kingdom of God as kingdom citizens? We need to return what we have been freely given by God. We need to sacrifice no matter the cost, serving and sacrificing even in the smallest things. Then we will experience amazing changes throughout the kingdom, and God's citizens will build up a beautiful culture of God's kingdom on earth.

10 ⊕ LOOK FAR AHEAD

Gamblers are typically impatient. By its very nature, gambling shows immediate results with success or failure, so chronic gamblers tend to be nervous and impatient. But is it only gamblers who are like this? From my observation, those who do not acknowledge God, looking only to people instead, seem to be restless and impetuous as well. Living with anxiety and impatience is to be nearsighted, marching down a zigzag path. However, when our eyes are focused on the Lord, and we are aware of only him, we are looking far ahead and following a straight path for our lives. It may seem slow at first, but just wait. The fruit will come.

Unfortunately, many pastors these days are impatient. They want to quickly reap the harvest from the gospel they are reading. Passion for the gospel is crucial, as is eagerness to spread the word to just one more person. However, we tend to use up all our energy in sharing the gospel, when we also need to save some of that energy for waiting patiently for results. It is, after all, the Holy Spirit who opens the hearts of the recipients. We are called to plant the seeds and wait for the fruit to come.

We also need to be patient and wise in the ways we share the gospel. The methods we use are very important. Is it effective to stand on the street corner shouting, "Jesus is the way to heaven. If you have no faith, you will go to hell!" to random people? We need to be flexible and careful to avoid being too forceful. The reality is that, today, most people will not even open the door if we knock with the intention of sharing the gospel. We are living in a new generation. We cannot run recklessly, trying to reach the goal faster. The right direction is more important than speed.

In today's society, it is more important to form the proper relationships. I am not trying to convince you to use the secular strategy of building relationships to build success and reach your goals. Rather, we need to show people the living God through our lifestyles and in our relationships to them—*before* we share the gospel with them. My life should be a witness to all that God is love, and my heart and attitude toward others should also reveal how great God's love is. On one hand this may seem time consuming, but it would be a more accurate, stronger witness of the gospel. And after some time, they may feel that they want to know more about this Jesus in whom we believe.

Pastors need to use this type of approach with their lives. If a pastor only focuses on preaching, leaving all the responsibility for evangelism to the members of the church, the old model of evangelism will continue. Pastors need to stand before everyone as a model of an evangelistic lifestyle and help guide the congregation through the sermons and discipleship, even though it may seem slow. Instead of handing out promotional fliers, seeking growth in numbers and hosting just a single evangelistic event, we need to teach the church to practice evangelism that is compelled by a love for lost souls.

Are you an impatient person? Use that to passionately pray through the Holy Spirit. Keep the faith in the God who dwells within us. If you completely believe in him, slow down a bit and approach lost souls with a prayerful heart, nurturing them along until they see God in us.

I came to this insight by reviewing the percentage of new members who settle in our church. We have a lot of new members coming into our church every year, but only 65 percent of them remain in the church. This percentage shows that we do a good job evangelizing people yet lack the continuous, nurturing action that brings them to genuinely meet the Lord. To solve this problem, our leaders and lay members are cooperating to strengthen the new-member care ministry in conjunction with the evangelism strategy I have shared. We are reminded that the most important thing is to have soul-saving hearts. We are continually learning as we move slowly, but I am sure the fruit of our efforts will eventually be harvested.

11 ● BEFORE BLAMING OTHERS

A priest in the cathedral of a small town was celebrating the Lord's Supper when the boy serving the priest accidentally dropped the cup of wine on the floor. The cup broke, and the wine spilled out. The priest was so upset that he slapped the servant boy on the cheek, shouting, "Never appear in front of the altar again!" The boy went home weeping. The boy's name was Josip Broz Tito. He later became president of Yugoslavia and was a famous dictator in their history.

In another cathedral, in a large city, a similar situation happened. The priest, however, kindly looked at the frightened boy and calmly said, "You will become a priest someday." That boy grew up to become a prominent archbishop named Fulton J. Sheen.

Even Jesus, after his resurrection, did not condemn his disciples for being weak or for hiding or for making mistakes. Rather, he encouraged them and gave them a mission, refreshing the disciples. And they, in turn, became powerful witnesses of his resurrection. Following Christ's example, we too need to be encouragers in order to help others understand our mission.

Appreciation is as important as encouragement. There once was a boy who was consistently naughty and did nothing that could be appreciated. One day the boy happened to clean up the bathroom quite well, and for the first time, his mother appreciated his contribution. A few days later the mother went to a parent-teacher meeting at the boy's school. She saw the lockers of the students decorated with posters depicting their dream jobs. She was surprised to see her son's locker with the word *janitor* on it.

The mother decided to compliment her son in order to reinforce her desire for him to study hard. She let him have extra tutoring for his English studies and continued to praise him for his efforts. One day, she found a line in his journal that said, "I will study English very hard!" She was delighted that her plan had been successful until she read further and saw, "I will study English hard to be a janitor in a big building in the U.S.!"

This is a humorous story, but it illustrates the powerful and long-lasting impact that our compliments can have. My associate pastors receive many of my compliments. They were all my students when I taught at KNU over a period of ten years, so I am familiar with their individual weaknesses. Yet I know that their weaknesses are not their problems alone. As their teacher, I am partly at fault, and I need to reflect on my own flaws before blaming others. I need to approach them with heartfelt responsibility. There are times when I must give critical advice and, on occasion, may need to rebuke them. But I am careful never to dissuade them from their call to ministry. I support them as they leave our church to go and plant another church, and I will never cease to support each one.

I continually encourage my assistant pastors, rather than command them, to voluntarily fulfill their duties—such as in attendance of dawn prayer worship. It is a fact that attending the dawn prayer service every morning is not easy for anyone. And occasionally the assistant pastors fail to attend them. But I never scold them for being absent because I remind myself of the times when I used to be unfaithful in my commitment to dawn prayer worship. The advice I give to my associate pastors who have a hard time making it to dawn prayer worship is, "If you miss now, you will have double the hardship later!"

I also make every effort to give them objective evaluations to lessen the chances of their being criticized by the congregation. As a pastor myself, I understand that it is significantly less painful to be evaluated by a coworker than by the members of the church. This is why I always step in and offer helpful advice before a problem arises. Yet I humbly confess that I still have a long way to go in my attitude toward my assistant pastors. There have been times, regrettably, when I blamed them for something when I should have been more encouraging. But I continue to make every effort to consider my own shortcomings before I reprove others. Encouragement and appreciation should always come before criticism.

12 ⊕ FIRST LOVE

In the book *Jesus in Blue Jeans*, Laurie Beth Jones tells a story of a duck that drowned. When Laurie was ten years old, she came home from school and found her favorite duck drowned in the pond. Her mother was shocked at the sad news. They called a veterinarian to find out how a duck could drown in a pond.

After the examination, the veterinarian said, "This duck was not able to take care of itself. The ducks have waterproofing oil discharged under their wings to paste all over their body. But it seems this duck failed to distribute the oil. I guess you overprotected the duck by having it in your house. Without the oil spread over its body, the duck could not float in water once it became wet, so it eventually drowned."

The spoiled duck made no effort to paste the waterproofing oil on its body to survive in the water. How does this story apply to our lives? How are our ministries doing? Have we quit being intentional?

Occasionally, there are times when I succumb to routines. In the year 2000, when I was first called to Sangamdong Church, my passions were on fire. But after some time, with the completion of the building project, along with the responsibilities of serving the community and supporting the small church, I found that I was spiritually exhausted. I asked myself, *Am I simply supervising the ministry?* At that stage of growth, this could be a typical reaction for pastors. However, we cannot continue in that pattern.

To get out of that cycle, I held onto one thing, and that was my first love. I had to remember my first love—the time when I had just started preaching. This may sound simple, but it was not easy to put into practice. I desperately needed God's intervention and grace.

Some may look for a new thing to help them get out of the cycle or challenge themselves to break free of the feelings. That may be beneficial for some. Yet I believe that going back to your first love and restarting the race is a more fundamentally sound approach. With this approach, we can be rejuvenated through the process of reflecting on our lives. The passion and eagerness of our first love will come alive in our hearts. And the purity of our first love will return to us.

I wish every ministry in our church would cling to its first love. It is my desire and wish for every church member to keep our first love. And my desire is that our first love, with its passion and purity, will be given to God even decades later.

13 ⊕ LOVE OTHERS AS THEY NEED

In *The 5 Love Languages*, Gary Chapman explains that we have five ways of expressing love to others and receiving love from others: words of affirmation, quality time, gifts, acts of service, and physical touch. These love languages do not apply to everyone to the same degree because everyone is different, and some people may express love by a different language than the one by which they prefer to receive love. Understanding the concept of the love languages helps us tailor the way we interact with people, whether in giving or receiving love. Love is better received when people are better understood.

Recently, a member of my congregation shared a story with me of his attempt to adopt a child. He shared that he had been rejected by the adoption agency due to his advanced age. The agency went on to explain that they prefer to find parents who are suitable to adopt the children rather than simply provide children for adoptive parents. I totally agree with this adoption agency's approach, and the church could learn from it. We need to find and focus on the needs of our church members, rather than simply supplying the leaders for the atmosphere of "the church."

Nowadays, in my country, you can see love slogans pasted around. Yet there is no guarantee that this love is genuine. I have performed many good deeds for others, but to be honest, many of those deeds may have been to satisfy myself rather than the other person. An example of this is seen in the relationship between parents and children in Korea. Many parents sacrifice greatly for their children's schooling, saying that the sacrifice is all for the child. Yet it seems that they are seeking a vicarious contentment for themselves rather than purely sacrificing for their children. They may think they are doing everything for their children, but they are actually promoting their own desires. These parents tell themselves that they have committed their entire lives for the happiness of their children in the name of love, but their children are not happy. When we respond to others only in the way we prefer, we are not acting in love.

In ministry, which requires a great amount of relational sensitivity, we need to be able to discern the needs of others and be sensitive enough to see their hearts. This requires observing and acknowledging their needs. Love grows when we ask what a person needs right now. Answering that question with a sympathetic heart and genuine concern for someone's well-being might be love itself. And that will become an expression of ministry and the very heart of a pastor.

Even churches are getting tired of the love slogans because we are content to misinterpret our sacrifices for our own benefit as sacrificing for others. When we put forth even a small effort toward others and that effort bears fruit, the congregation will feel the warmth of our love. Moreover, the marginalized people in our neighborhoods will be knocking at the doors of our churches.

14 ⊕ THIS TOO SHALL PASS

If our point of view were to be changed, everything would look different. If we wore dark sunglasses, everything we looked at would be dark, or if we wore red-tinted glasses, everything would seem rosy. Likewise, our thoughts and emotions will dictate the way we see things.

Once there were two frogs that fell into a deep puddle. The other frogs nearby called to the two frogs and told them that the puddle was too deep, that they would never be able to get out, and that they would surely die there. One of the frogs felt defeated by this news, and he soon drowned. The other frog, however, was not dissuaded by the comments from his frog friends, and with great effort he was able to get out of the puddle.

The frogs in the group that had gathered around said to him, "Didn't you hear us shouting that there was no way out and you would die?"

The surviving frog answered, "I must be hard of hearing. I thought you were cheering me on!"

Of course, the frog actually did hear the others discouraging him, but he chose to ignore their worthless mocking and, amazingly, survived. The two frogs in the puddle heard the same taunts from the other frogs, but they received the taunts with completely different attitudes. Likewise, the joy in our lives may depend on our point of view!

"Looking back, my life seems like one long obstacle race—with me as the chief obstacle," said Jack Paar, a famous American author and comedian. More crucial than an obstacle itself is actually our viewpoint toward the obstacle. Depending on the way we look at it, we can either overcome or be defeated by the same crisis. Our perception and attitudes are of utmost importance. I continually encourage my congregation to have a positive outlook because, no matter how difficult the situation, one can overcome. Of course, I understand that their lives may, at times, be more challenging than my own. People come to church seeking divine intervention, peace, and healing—only to face greater challenges when they go back to their daily lives. I gently encourage them with the wisdom that this too shall pass.

There is a saying from the Hebrew *Midrash* texts. King David, as is well known, was a strong warrior who won battles everywhere he went. One day, he asked his wise man to make him a ring that would keep him humble in victory and encouraged in defeat. The wise man, after trying unsuccessfully to come up with the right words, went to a wise prince in Israel named Solomon and asked for his help. Solomon gave him the words for King David's ring: *This too shall pass!*

No matter what it is, it will pass away with time. In moments of great happiness, when it seems the joy and bright future might stretch on forever, you will find it is only temporary. Therefore there is no reason to be proud, boastful, or look down on others as inferior to ourselves because the moment will pass. Likewise, there is nothing to be in anguish or miserable about because the bad things too will eventually pass. "This too shall pass" is my encouragement to everyone. Wear these sunglasses to see things differently in your life. Inscribe this ring on your mind. Remember that the only one we should look to is our Lord.

15 ⊕ FORGIVE FIRST

A sick child's parents took him to the hospital, where he was diagnosed with a malignant tumor. The doctor prescribed chemotherapy treatment. A little ways into the chemotherapy, the child had a seizure and died. The subsequent investigation found that the child died of an overdose. He had been given ten times the proper chemotherapy dosage. The doctor confessed his fault, expecting the parents to explode in anger.

Surprisingly, the parents calmly listened to the doctor and then said, "We really appreciate that you did your best to save our son's life. We are sure he is in heaven now with Jesus. Please do not be upset about what happened."

They did not yell or threaten the doctor with a lawsuit. They were simply convinced that their child was with the Lord. Their attitude deeply moved the doctor, and he eventually became a Christian. Later in life, he succeeded his father as the leader of a non-government organization. The doctor's name is John Templeton. His NGO, the Templeton Foundation, awards and encourages religious achievers and helps the needy. The Templeton Award given by this foundation is known as the Nobel Prize of religious circles. Mother Teresa, Rev. Billy Graham, and the late Rev. Kyungjik Han, one of the earliest and most respected Korean pastors, are among the recipients of this award. This story demonstrates the power of genuine Christian forgiveness that brings about new life.

Nobel Prize-winning professor and author Gabriel Garcia Marquez shares a story in his book *Love in the Time of Cholera*. The story is about a wife who forgot to replace the soap in the bathroom. When her husband went in to take a shower and found no soap, he became angry and shouted, "I have been showering for more than a week without any soap!"

The wife was irritated and yelled back at him, "What, more than a week? You're exaggerating!"

After the argument, they did not communicate with each other for seven months. They slept in separate rooms and did not speak at the dinner table.

Was it just a bar of soap that caused the problems between them? Or did it perhaps have more to do with the fact that people find it difficult to apologize at an intimate level?

My wish is that all of God's people experience the healing power of forgiveness and voluntarily forgive others. We must remember that we are commanded by Jesus to forgive others. Were we not freely forgiven by the blood Jesus shed on the cross?

We are called to forgive seventy times seven, no matter what the sin was. "Then Peter came to Jesus and asked, 'Lord, how many times shall I forgive my brother or sister who sins against me? Up to seven times?' Jesus answered, 'I tell you, not seven times, but seventy-seven times'" (Matthew 18:21–22).

Let us reflect on our own lives. No one is without sin, but God forgives when we repent of our sins. God cleanses our sin and does not remember it anymore. Let us remember our God who never stops loving us, even when we sin.

It is not easy to forgive those who sin against us. On our own, it is difficult to forgive. We may intend to forgive someone, but the next time we see that person we are reminded again of the hurt. This is why it is important that emotional forgiveness accompany intentional forgiveness. Intentionally forgiving is making up our minds to forgive, while emotional forgiveness is digging deep down into our hearts to forgive whenever the memory pops up. It takes time to genuinely forgive others. Agony and regret will, surprisingly, turn into joy and happiness.

16 ⊕ DEPRESSION, FRIENDS, AND FIRM RELATIONSHIPS

Depression is a deadly disease. They say that 15 percent of people suffering from depression will attempt suicide. This mortality rate is serious! We all have witnessed through the media the number of celebrities who end up committing suicide because of depression. What makes it so serious is that everyone is exposed to this disease.

How, then, do we keep from becoming depressed? Certainly there isn't a cure-all that will work for everyone, but one way is to encourage healthy relationships with others. There is a saying that "a man who finds a friend who understands him will never try to take his own life." To a certain degree, we are responsible for finding and maintaining strong relationships with those who understand us. Friendship does not just happen. I need to be a good friend continually to others in order to keep people around me who want to be good friends to me. In other words, I will *have* good friends when I *become* a good friend. Even husbands and wives who vowed at their weddings to be there for each other can become strangers if they do not intentionally strive to care for each other.

With the awareness that depression can strike anyone, we need to strive to keep good relationships with the friends in our everyday lives. Having friends is not solely for pleasure or entertainment. Genuine friends are willing to share each other's burdens and happiness and to lend a hand when needed.

What, then, is required to maintain good friendships? What must we consistently do to retain friendships? There are many options but one consistent theme: We must watch our words. Friendships are built on conversations. Yet we see people being hurt by what their friends say to them, and the relationship is damaged and not restored. Keep in mind that the majority of damage to relationships is caused by the tongue. Those who tend to hurt others with their verbal attacks typically do not realize what they are saying or how their words affect the other person. The one who was verbally attacked suffers long after, while the one who said the unkind words has no idea of the damage caused. The argumentative person may often have a history of harsh or violent language. They could simply be repeating what they heard growing up and not be aware of the impact their malicious words have on others.

When we are offended by what someone says to us, we should try to understand why these people are that way. It can be helpful to remember that those who irritate others with their words are not wicked by nature. We need to attempt to understand them not only for their sakes but also for the sake of our own emotional healing. We need to think about how the other person was raised: Were they brought up on a bed of roses? We all should develop a so-called immunity toward harsh words because no one has control over another person's tongue, so it is wise if we guard our own hearts.

First, focus on the message itself rather than the expression of the speaker. In every situation, we need to understand the content of the message. Even if the speaker was demeaning or critical, ask yourself twice, *Does he or she intend to hurt me?* Most of the time we will conclude that they are not intending to hurt but are, rather, blurting out thoughtlessly. You can then erase from your mind, without any thought, what you heard. Of course, it does take quite a bit of time, self-discipline, and character-building to be able to control your mind in this type of situation. But this is an effective way to protect yourself from verbal attack.

Second, seek to understand the background of the speaker. If you truly empathize with this person and are genuinely concerned with understanding them, you will likely receive the message less hurtfully. Keep in mind that a harsh tone may not have anything to do with a person's feelings toward you; it could be that it has simply become an unconscious habit for the other person. You may even feel sympathy, understanding that they might be in a frustrating situation and feel compelled to speak this way.

Third, forgive the person, but more than that, bless them—even if the situation feels unforgivable. In his book *An Ambassador of God*, Ha Joong Kim, a Korean ambassador, wrote that he used to post the names of the people who slandered him in visible places—such on his desk or near the toilet. His intent, of course, was to remind himself to bless these people and not curse them. He testified in his book that the negative feelings would not even enter his mind when he automatically blessed those names whenever his eyes saw the names.

This kind of coping strategy would be commendable for every Christian. We receive criticism in the church as well as in the workplace. But these words will not hurt you as much if you respond by blessing the person. Remember, the Bible tells us to "bless those who persecute you; bless and do not curse" (Romans 12:14). If your faith is simple, your response will be simple as well. If your faith is complex, your life gets complex too! As the Bible tells us to bless others, our only response can simply be to obey—and bless them.

This kind of attitude represents the level of our self-esteem. The ability to read the real message of the speaker shows our true character and dignity. This will not be easy; it will be a challenge for anyone. There may be several factors in building relationships with others, but let us keep in mind how we should respond to the unkind words of others. In so doing we will be able to put forth the effort required to build strong friendships.

17 ⊕ THE LANGUAGE OF CHRISTIANS

Abraham Lincoln's father was a shoemaker. When Lincoln was elected president of the United States, all the aristocrats were disturbed by the fact that he was from the lower social class. Just before Lincoln was to give his inaugural address, an old congressman stood up and said, "Mr. Lincoln, although by some accident you have become the president of our country, don't forget that you used to come with your father to my house to prepare shoes for my family. And there are many senators who are wearing the shoes made by your father." The people started to laugh and mock him.

But Abraham Lincoln was not irritated by the comment. Rather, he responded with a smile and said, "Sir, I know that my father used to make shoes in your house for your family, and there will be many others here—because nobody else can make shoes the way he did. He was a creator. He poured his soul into it. I want to ask you, have you any complaint? Because I know how to make shoes myself; if you have any complaint I can make you another pair of shoes. But as far as I know, nobody has ever complained about my father's shoes. He was genius, a great creator, and I am proud of my father."

At his gentle response, no one could say another word. How about us? Can we respond gently when people make slanderous comments about us? Or are we more like the aristocrats in Abraham Lincoln's life, hurting others with our harsh tongues?

Here is a similar story that was introduced in the book *Cafeteria for the Soul*, by Stephanie Bender-Leggett: There once lived a talkative woman in Israel. She realized her endless gossip was causing problems among the people of the village and also in her own family, so she went to a rabbi to ask for help.

The rabbi lit a candle and asked her what she would need to do to the flame in order to be able to use the candle.

She said nothing needed to be done with it; rather, she should let it be.

The rabbi told her it was the same with her tongue. The best approach is not to do anything with it and just let it be.

The Bible says, "Anyone who is never at fault in what they say is perfect . . ." (James 3:2b).

As surely as backbiting, slander, and gossip are intended to hurt people, words of respect, compliments, and attentive listening will dissolve all kinds of problems. The ability to communicate verbally is one of the greatest gifts God has given us, and it is the key to building human relationships.

We cannot control what others say, only what we ourselves say. We need to be cautious with our words and careful when giving advice to others. We need to consider responding in pleasant ways. These efforts will be valuable to us personally and even more as Christians.

In my country, there were recent stories on the news about people who yell vicious words at random passengers on public transportation. They are called "subway maligners." Sadly, the abusive language usually escalated to physical violence as well.

Words can cause such fury. My very words can trigger unpredictable rage in others. However, we can also cultivate peaceful environments through our words. A community that is peaceful instead of angry depends on the words of its leader. Remembering the power and authority of our words, let us discipline ourselves to control our tongues.

18 ⊕ THE BEST GIFT

Children are a wonderful gift from God. For this reason, we parents should be reminded of God whenever we look at our children. We should be thankful that God has given us such a wonderful gift and also thankful for who they are. Through our life's pilgrimage on this earth, we are blessed by the joy and happiness that our children bring us. The Bible says, "Man that is in honor, and understandeth not, is like the beasts that perish" (Psalm 49:20, KJV). If we do not recognize that our children are precious gifts from God, then we are like the beasts that perish.

Parents, especially in competitive urban societies, need to examine their hearts to see if they really love their children just as they are. Unfortunately, many parents in my country tend to have high expectations for the academic level of their children. They put added stress and burdens on their children by requiring them to study unreasonable amounts. We hear stories of parents being anxious themselves on the day the child receives a school report card. What do you think would happen to those parents if the child were to receive almost all Fs, with just one D, on the report card? The parents would probably be terribly upset. Many Korean parents may even go as far as to argue with each other over whom the child takes after. However, as Christians who believe that our children are an inheritance that God has entrusted to us, we should have a different approach. We might say something like, "Next time, I would like to see you put more effort in those other subjects, as I see you have done better in the one subject." We need to regard our children as beloved, regardless of their learning abilities. When we look at our children, we need to remember that God created them and that they are the most precious gift God has given us.

As we know, Abraham in the Old Testament was abundantly blessed by God. Two different kings were even jealous of Abraham's possessions and his beautiful wife. Yet Abraham was not content with all these things. He wanted an heir. When he was finally given a son at the age of one hundred, he was overjoyed. This shows what a blessing from heaven our children are.

The greatest gift we parents can hand down to our children is a legacy of Christian faith. With this in mind, I would ask every Christian parent not to pressure their children so much over their secular education that their religious education suffers. There should be no compromise in teaching our religious legacy to our children.

I have a friend who is currently a professor at a university. He used to be a real character and always had poor grades in school. His mother was a faithful Christian, however, and she was not nearly as concerned about his grades in school as she was about him missing church. Every time she found out he had missed church, she punished him severely. He even shared a story about how once, when she was so upset he had missed church again because he had been hanging around his non-Christian friends, she hit him in the head with a frying pan.

He is now a totally different person. He studied hard enough that he was able to go to the U.S. to obtain his degrees and became a professor. Moreover, he has a very important position in his school. Although the way his mother disciplined him was extreme, I believe he was fortunate to have a mother who consistently instructed him in the right way to live. Because of his mother, who never compromised her faith and values, he was able to overcome his struggles and glorify the name of God.

Sadly, I see parents in my country who ask their children who are high school seniors to study instead of attend church so they can pass their college entrance exams. These parents may be faithful church members themselves, but their priorities are mixed up if they value schoolwork over Christian faith.

These days there are a number of families whose parents both work. Since they do not have enough time to see to their children's studies themselves, they send their children to afterschool programs for private tutoring. In actuality children's academic achievements reflect their own efforts, not the concern or support of their parents. Sending them to a learning center does not guarantee a good result. Let us rather direct our concern to our children's relationship with God rather than to their schoolwork. Even in a busy family with both parents working, children can be well nurtured spiritually.

Some may say that I am unrealistic about this, but as an educator, I am very aware of and sensitive to the realities of today's education demands. Nonetheless, I maintain that spiritual discipline should come first in a child's education. Once they meet the Lord, our worries are over. Even though our children may seem unsure about their futures or lacking in their schoolwork, we should focus on guiding them to meet Jesus as their personal Savior rather than forcing them to throw themselves into their studies. Allow children to regularly worship the Lord and be nurtured through the Word of God. By encouraging rather than forcing them, we may lead them by grace closer to the Lord. Our desire is that our children would meet and experience God on a personal level that would transform their lives. This might encourage them to study harder in order to glorify the name of Jesus. Once they grasp their godly mission, they will have a clear vision and goal for their lives.

If this is your desire for your children, then start now. Do not feel guilty for your firm discipline. Some parents who are both working feel guilty they are not able to spend enough time with their children and thus tend to be lenient even when firm discipline is called for. They should not be reluctant to be stern and fair in their spiritual discipline. When a mother works outside the home to support the family, that does not mean she is not loving or caring for her children appropriately, so she should not be hesitant or feel bad about strictly guiding and disciplining. Mothers, be confident in your nurturing and also in your disciplining of your children because this is the best gift you can give to them.

19 ⊕ HONEST BEFORE GOD

These days it seems that many parents expect the church to be fully responsible for the spiritual growth of their children. Christian education is not only accomplished in the church but also in the community and in the family. Overall, both the family and the church are essential in forming a child's Christian faith. Considering that children spend more time at home with their families than they do in the church, they should be following the model of their parents. This explains why the children in the church may have different attitudes about Christian education. In other words, children who grow up in families devoted to prayer might grow up to be prayer warriors themselves. Or children who grow up in families who love the Word of God might grow up loving to read the Bible. In the same way, children who grow up in families with a negative religious influence may have a hard time with spiritual growth.

The firm faith of a Christian shows in a solid life. A solid Christian has a solid character. Sometimes we see a faithful church member who exhibits poor relationships with others. This may be because their faith was not formed in a healthy way. When we are on the right path in our faith journeys, our lives are continually being transformed. With this in mind, parents should strive to be good examples to their children.

Among the many values that Christian parents should teach their children, honesty should be emphasized. Honesty is also valued in secular education. I am not talking just about the integrity that is expected by the world, but an honest life is living righteously before God—that is, *coram Deo*.

Once I served as an associate pastor in a church in the city of Pyeongtaek while living in Cheonan. My wife and I attended the morning service at 11:00 a.m., but my son rode the public bus to attend the children's church service that began at 8:00 a.m. One day my son excitedly told his mother that he knew how to get to Pyeongtaek for half the normal bus fare. He explained that the bus always stopped halfway between Cheonan and Pyeongtaek. According to him, the bus conductor never checked the tickets at the halfway mark, so he began purchasing tickets to the half-way mark instead of to his actual destination, Pyeongtaek. He was very proud of himself, traveling twice the distance with a ticket at half the fare.

My wife did not lose her temper with him or punish him. After listening to his story she just cried, tears running down her face. She was heartbroken by his dishonesty and misplaced pride. Seeing the tears of his mother, my son knew something was wrong and truly repented of what he had done. Through this situation, my wife was able to reemphasize honesty to our son, and he never failed to obey his mother in this regard. He would rather be called boring than dishonest.

A story of what happened to him while he was studying in Boston illustrates this change in his character. He was attending a Korean church and met a friend who had come to church two or three times. The two of them shopped at a Korean grocery store together several times after church. The boy then stopped coming. After a few months, the owner of the Korean grocery store asked my son if he remembered the guy who had come with him a few months earlier. He explained that the boy had been purchasing groceries on credit and still owed him $650, and he wanted to know if my son knew how to contact him.

For a young student studying abroad, $650 is a large amount of money. My son had been praying for his friend to come back to church and to grow spiritually. After hearing that he had snuck away, leaving a debt of $650, my son felt deeply troubled. To my surprise, my son found a part-time job and earned $650 over a three-month period to pay back the store owner what his friend owed him. He could have just ignored the debt of this friend—it wasn't his problem, after all—but he felt a holy burden about it.

He did not want the store owner to have any negative prejudice about Christians. My son may not be perfect, but he wanted to demonstrate to others that Christians are honest people.

My son, who once tricked the bus conductor, became a person of honesty and integrity because of his mother's persistent teaching. If we teach our children to be honest before God, they will not do shameful things in their lives. They will be good role models for others even with their imperfections. My prayer is that all Christian families teach the power of honesty to their children because I believe a person who is honest before God will lead a righteous life. Christian education that values honesty will build up righteous Christians and their communities.

20 ⊕ THE CHURCH'S RESPONSIBILITY FOR ITS CHILDREN

A lot of children in my country dream about becoming celebrities when they grow up. They spend a lot of time following the younger celebrity stars and so-called idols. They believe popularity automatically leads to fame, power, and money. With this type of dream, the children are in danger of putting themselves above God. They are seeking the praise of visible people, rather than that of the invisible God. Those who run after fame are doomed to fall into despair when the fame fades away.

Similar problems are also common among teenagers. The deep-rooted problems, such as juvenile delinquency, violence, and bullying are all growing from year to year, with newly evolving problems, due to the absence of moral discipline. The environment in the schools seems to be high dollar and high fashion, with defiant attitudes. Teachers have lost their authority. Students snap at teachers and notify the police if a teacher takes disciplinary action. We even hear of students committing acts of violence against teachers. In this highly competitive society, our children are becoming more selfish.

In response to this reality, the church has a responsibility to take care of these children. What can be done to help them learn and develop righteous values? Is there a way for the church to do this? Unfortunately, our church does not yet have a strong children's department, for which I feel bad. Worse than that, many youth miss worship, citing academic burdens as an excuse. I know there are still a small number of those students who love to worship and listen to the Word. I am delighted to see them refreshed and strengthened in the Lord, even in the midst of their academic competition to enter college. I pray that more of them will come to the church to be filled.

One special feature of our youth department (for middle and high school students) is that they join the adult worship service with their parents on Sunday mornings and listen to the same message. They do not have a separate youth worship service. But, after the service with their parents, they are encouraged to come to small group sessions for further discussion. My rationale for doing this is to embrace the youth in the regular worship service without the unnecessary transition that would happen later on. From my observation, almost 90 percent of children drop out of church when they enter middle school. And this dramatic decline is not so much different than when they graduate from high school. Sad to say, this is the reality of Korean churches these days.

For this reason, I invite the youth to join our adult worship service. That way, since they are used to being in the service, they do not have any adjustment period when they graduate from high school. I adopted this model from Geumran Methodist Church in Korea.

Earlier, I emphasized the significance of spiritual discipline in the family. But the church is also obligated to help this growing generation be spiritually nurtured. I am not certain that this model is the best way to fulfill this obligation, but I am sure we will continue to improve and find better ways as we go along. It is our prayer that all of our children personally meet the Lord and grow as men and women of God. Although we do not run exciting programs for our youth like some churches, our focus is to help them stand firm on the Word of God and live accordingly. After all, children and youth will be adults some day. No one knows exactly what they will be or what they will do, but one thing is for sure: The church will be responsible for their lives.

21 ⊕ BEAUTIFUL SACRIFICE OF COUPLES

It is said that men and women live in different time periods. Johann Wolfgang von Goethe said, "Women live a life based on the past while men live a life led by the future. Women are to be viewed through a microscope while men should be viewed through a telescope."

This statement simply shows the difference between men and women. Problems arise when a man of the future and a woman of the past live together in modern times. Conflicts and misunderstandings can occur between a husband and wife because they do not understand that their time frames are different from each other. When a wife always talks about things from the past, the husband is annoyed with his wife for dwelling on the past. However, the wife has a hard time reconciling with her husband when he simply moves forward without correcting past mistakes. This is why couples need to make every effort to understand each other. Couples will find true happiness when they learn to look at situations from the other person's viewpoint.

A pastor and close friend of mine shared this story. One year their wedding anniversary fell on a Sunday. After a long day at church with the Sunday service and fellowship, the pastor planned to take his wife to a nice restaurant to show his appreciation of her sacrificial life. On the way to the restaurant, however, his wife pointed out a mistake from his sermon earlier that day. Well aware of the mistake and unhappy about it himself, the pastor got upset and turned the car around to go home without a word. They did not say anything to each other on the drive home. But soon the pastor began feeling bad about his actions and was considering what he could do to break the silence between them.

At the door of the parsonage, their dog welcomed them with a wagging tail. In an attempt to break the awkwardness, he said, "Honey, our kin is welcoming us; why don't you respond to him?"

She said to the dog in a serious tone, "How are you doing, my father-in-law?"

After a moment, both husband and wife burst into uncontrollable laughter.

This sort of thing can happen to anyone. But disagreements become less important when we accept each other with open hearts. Sacrifice is needed between a husband and wife. With open minds in every situation, they must accept each other's differences.

Words are dangerously powerful in human relationships, especially between married couples. For it is with our words that we express the feelings in our hearts. Unfortunately, I see a lot of married couples in my country speaking to each other disrespectfully, even though they surely were in love when they married years ago. They even seem comfortable speaking to each other so carelessly.

The Korean language carries two distinctive linguistic registers, and I maintain that spouses should use the honorific form of speech, not the casual form with each other. Using the casual form of speech may bond the couple closely like old friends but may also put the other person down unintentionally. The casual form of speech sounds commanding when asking for something, such as, "Bring me water!" or, "Do this!" However, the honorific form sounds very different as the requests become, "Please give me water" or, "Would you please do this?"

Years ago, a couple who had a problem with arguing came to see me. I offered a simple solution—to change the way they speak to each other. I asked if they were willing to commit themselves to what I suggested for six months. They both agreed, so I gave them some homework. They were to control the form of speech they used with each other. They made a chart to check off how many times they used honorific or casual forms of speech with each other on a daily basis. They confessed that it was really hard at first; they felt like their tongues were twisted out of control. I urged them very strongly to continue with the exercise, and gradually they changed the way they spoke to each other and fixed their problems.

Words have power. I wish that all husbands and wives would learn how to make good use of the power of their words. Christian couples especially are to be models for others in keeping peace in the family by using appropriate words.

22 ⊕ THE HOLY SPIRIT'S CHURCH

"This is mine because I made it!" said a little boy, merrily floating a toy boat he had made attached to a string in his hand. The boat floated peacefully here and there on the lake. But one day a storm came and took the string right out of the boy's hand. His boat slowly disappeared from sight. The boy was very sad about losing his favorite boat.

A few months later, a toy sitting on the shelf in a toy store caught his attention. *What on earth is that?* he thought and stepped closer to the window. It was the very boat he had lost months ago. He was so excited and went into the shop and explained to the owner what happened to him.

But the owner of the shop said, "I am sorry, my dear, but this belongs to me now. Come back with your money if you want to have it back."

The boy was determined and saved his allowance until he finally had enough to purchase the boat. Holding the boat in his arms with a big smile, the boy said, "You are mine, two times. The first time, you were mine because I made you. Now you are mine because I bought you."

God says the same thing to us. God made us and then bought us. How, then, should we respond? In what ways can we serve the God who is both our Creator and owner? Surrendering ourselves to the Lord as our owner means that we invite the Holy Spirit as our owner as well.

With this in mind, my goal for Sangamdong Church was to give ownership to the Holy Spirit. Ministry is not led by ministers; they are just the tools the Holy Spirit uses to lead. What would it look like to have a church owned and ministered to by the Holy Spirit? The church led by the Holy Spirit would be transformational. The Holy Spirit approaches individuals' lives with the right words, in the right place, at the right time. Even though the same message is preached to everyone in the service, the Holy Spirit speaks to individuals in different ways. Sometimes the Spirit touches their broken hearts and other times leads them to repentance, guiding them to the right direction for their lives. Most importantly, the church led by the Holy Spirit clearly bears the nine fruits of the spirit—love, joy, peace, patience, kindness, goodness, faithfulness, gentleness, and self-control—as evidence of the Spirit's working. Ministry that is directed by the plans and power of a human leader brings conflict and problems, while ministry led by the Holy Spirit will bear the fruit of the Spirit, which will encourage everyone.

This kind of ministry is not limited to influence within the church but extends also to the community. When the members of the church are transformed by the work of the Holy Spirit, the church becomes powerful and inevitably respected among other organizations in the community, just as the early Christians in the first era suffered persecution yet were held in high regard by others.

As we give control of the church to the Holy Spirit, my hope for Sangamdong Church is that people in the community will say, "People get changed when they go to Sangamdong Church!" or, "Do you know so-and-so? He is a totally different person now that he has joined Sangamdong Church!" With the help of the Holy Spirit, the church can serve the community better and stand firm as a strong congregation.

This may seem like a lofty dream to some, but it is more than true that when people with low self-esteem, depression, or low self-confidence meet the Holy Spirit, they can be transformed into people of God who can live holy lives boldly standing against the world. This is possible through the world of the Holy Spirit in the church. The Holy Spirit is the reason this seemingly unprecedented dream can be conceivable.

Our church has been striving to be recognized as a good church in our community by serving the community and sharing with its people. In the future, I am confident that we will be depending on the work of the Holy Spirit even more closely. I pray that the Spirit will be the one and only owner of our church and will raise up the church as a great model to others.

23 ⊕ HAPPINESS IS NEAR

One of the stories I read as a child was *The Blue Bird*, by Maurice Maeterlinck. As you may know, it is about a dream that Mytyl and Tyltyl, two children of a poor woodcutter, dream on Christmas Eve. In the dream, they meet an old fairy who puts green hats on them and asks them to find the blue bird of happiness. In their dream, the children wander the world searching for the blue bird but return home with nothing in their hands. When the children wake from the dream, they realize that the bird of happiness was the bird in their own cage.

This story teaches the important lesson that happiness is all around us, not just far away. Happiness is not just grand things; it could be an encouraging word when spouses part for the day. This concept applies to ministry as well. We are not supposed to search for happiness elsewhere; it can be found close by. It could be with the neighbors around us.

Sangamdong Church was fairly small with a congregation of about sixty members thirteen years go and has since grown to about twenty times that many members. One of the reasons for that amount of growth is the strategy of lifestyle evangelism that came from the idea that the church is useless if it is not recognized by the community where it is located. The church needs to serve the community prior to making an attempt to invite people from the community to church.

I promoted this method in our church. Lifestyle evangelism embraces the belief that the church is not only a place for worship but also for setting a good example of sacrificial service, as in caring for the underprivileged in the community. In doing this, not only those you serve will reap the rewards, but as you serve you will find true happiness in your giving of yourself to others.

This is a win-win system, and is not just an attempt to look good in front of others.

The blueprints of lifestyle evangelism were laid out in our church building project that was completed in October of 2003. When the building was under construction, the surrounding area was barren, unlike the way it is now with hundreds of buildings crowded around. The ground floor of the church building was designated as a preschool; the second floor was the main sanctuary and ministry-related offices; the third floor was a "silver school" for the elderly; the fourth floor was a physical therapy center; and the fifth floor was a cafeteria. Other than the second floor, which housed the sanctuary and offices, all others were to take care of those who are easily neglected in society. As the building was completed, these auxiliary organizations started operation right away, providing spaces to the neighbors who needed special care. This church has never stopped in its service to develop this community in various ministry areas, like nursery school, kindergarten, Sangamdong Nazarene Therapy Center (SNTC) for disabled children, Silver School for elders, and others. This has helped give the community a good impression of the church.

As we seek to support the residents of the community in areas of welfare, accommodation, and healthy social development by serving and sharing with them, we have created a financially challenging situation for the church. Thankfully, however, we have been well supported by our own members as well as through the minimal-level tuition paid by participants. As a result, we are getting two birds with one stone—instilling happiness in them and in ourselves. Through our continual investment in the residents of the community, the church was gradually recognized as representing what church is all about in the community, enjoying the happiness of a symbiotic relationship between the church and the community. Although investing a considerable portion of the church budget in the business of social welfare is hardly profitable, we are dedicated to this ministry. Service does not always have an evangelistic component. We believe that service to children, the disabled, and the elderly is the work our church should be doing.

Happiness does not exist only in the future. If we dream of reaching our nation and beyond, we must start by giving a hand to our closest neighbors. Remember that a happy church will produce happy citizens and, eventually, a happy society.

24 ⊕ A NOISY CHURCH IS A SERVANT CHURCH

Dr. Hyesung Cheon, author of *Servant Parents Raise up their Children with Greater Love,* is a mother of six children, all of whom have graduated from Harvard or Yale. Among them, Dr. Howard Kyongju Koh, her eldest son, served as the United States assistant secretary for health in the Obama administration from 2009 until 2014. Dr. Harold Hongju Koh, her third son, was the U.S. State Department's legal adviser from 2009 until 2013 and the dean of Yale Law School from 2004 until 2009. Dr. Cheon, known as a wise mother, introduces in the book "seven traits of 'traditional leadership' that twenty-first century leaders should be equipped with." At the very core of these traits is servant leadership.

Dr. Cheon and her late husband always emphasized to their children that morality and servanthood should go beyond the capacity one is born with. What they mean by morality is to consider others before yourself and to seek the public benefit—in other words, servanthood. The more capacity, the more morality should follow, and then others will follow your lead when your morality is testified beyond your capacity.

Surely, servanthood is critical in human relationships. The place where servanthood should be most active is in the church. With the task given to us to lead the world to the Lord, we must lead by serving, just as our Lord Jesus showed us.

What, then, would a servant church look like? To put it simply, it is noisy—not because its people are arguing or because of broken relationships but because it is busy with people serving and being served. It is going to be noisy where there is servanthood because we serve people. If I were to perform this task myself, it would be humble and quiet, but with many people serving one another, there is noise.

The publisher of *The Pulpit,* a well-known religious journal, once said, "A living church is always noisy with the chattering of children and youth while a dead church is dead silent." Sangam-dong Church values noise. It should not only be noisy on Sundays but also on every day during the week from Monday to Saturday as well. We encourage church members, young and old, to come to the church any time, on any day, just as they would to their homes. Although it is important to keep our sanctuary clean, it is not right to leave it empty all week. Considering that the church building was constructed with precious offerings from church members, how can we close the door and keep it only for ourselves? If there are continual footsteps in the church building, though it will be worn out faster, it will bear real beauty.

Those who enter our doors are greatly diverse. If you take a closer look, you will see they are the isolated neighbors who need special care. From little children in the nursery school, to the elderly in the Silver School, to the disabled children and their parents visiting our therapy center, I want to see our church even busier with more people. I do not want to leave the church empty for even a short period of time.

We used to keep our church open twenty-four hours a day in order for everyone to visit at whatever time was convenient for them. Unfortunately, we no longer leave it open that long ever since someone came to the church and smoked in the bathroom, nearly causing a fire. We now close between midnight and four o'clock in the morning. Other than those few hours, everyone is welcome and can stay as long as they need.

In Matthew 5:13–14, Jesus says, "You are the salt of the earth. But if the salt loses its saltiness, how can it be made salty again? It is no longer good for anything, except to be thrown out and trampled underfoot. You are the light of the world. A town built on a hill cannot be hidden." We need to be the salt and light, and in order to do so, we need to be among the people. Without the people, the salt and light are useless. As a servant church, as the salt and light, let us open the doors of the church wide.

At first people may not step in because of their religious prejudice. They may not want to be involved in any religious activities.
However, genuine servanthood will open their minds. As we bear
the heart of Jesus, who exemplified true servanthood, others will
taste the salt and see the light, which will eventually lead them to
the church. Having people registered as members is not the goal.
As we introduce others to the love of Christ in a place called a
church, then we have success.

25 ⊕ MINISTRY TO THE ELDERLY: SILVER SCHOOL

Psychologist Harry Harlow conducted the so-called "monkey love" experiment in the 1950s. He presented two kinds of surrogate mothers for infant monkeys. Both surrogates were made of cold wire, but one was covered with terrycloth while the other was left bare with just the milk bottle hanging from its body. After being fed from the bottle, the monkeys did not stay to hang around the cold-wire surrogate but clung to the terrycloth surrogate for large amounts of time. This interesting experiment proved that even animals are more attracted to softness.

This truth may apply in the same way to humans. Being cold as metal and sharp as a razor makes one lonely. People naturally seek friends who are tender and gentle, rather than cold and stern. People who are gentle and have a tender way are likely to have many friends. If we respond to others with gentleness, even tense relationships are soothed and will eventually bring peace and love.

We need to treat everyone we encounter with this approach. People expect Christians to treat them with gentleness, and we need to give special attention to the elderly with this approach. Most of us by nature treat children with kindness and gentleness. It is not easy to be unkind to an adorable little one. Young people receive appropriate treatment in society because of their freshness, youth, and capability. The situation is different when it comes to the elderly. People hesitate to interact with them and don't befriend them readily. Some even consider them annoying, so the elderly life becomes lonely. They greatly miss gentle words and warm eye contact. With the rapidly changing urban life, their aging appearance tends to make them feel degraded to the isolated class of society.

Sangamdong Church was aware of this issue and tried to find ways to provide the elderly with continued educational programs with a Christian approach. Through the Silver School, we attempt to meet their needs. Our church had a number of programs to serve the elderly, and I know they were helpful and a comfort for them in a way. Yet we needed more consistent programs than once-a-year events, which often just highlighted their loneliness. Our goal was not just to serve them temporarily but consistently and regularly.

Not surprisingly, Silver School did not start fully equipped. We began when we were still renting space for our church. We purchased two heating medical instruments that are known to be effective in treating neuralgia. We paid about $1,800 for each, and that was not cheap for a church of only sixty members! Back then, a lot of people moved out of Sangamdong because it was under the city's renovation project. This exodus left the ground floor of our building empty, so the owner of the building allowed us to use it rent-free. We had the two instruments and a room, so we invited the elderly in the community to come every day. Previously they had to travel to other districts on the public bus to enjoy free medical treatment. We advertised our free-of-charge services plus the benefit that they did not need to travel as far.

More than anything, we of course wished to win their souls to Christ, but I convinced the volunteers not to force them to come to church. We asked volunteers to serve them medical therapy along with some of their favorite refreshments. Gradually the news spread throughout the community, and we were able to open Silver School. Nine members were in the first batch, and now there are more than 150 who regularly attend. Starting as a small community service with just two medical instruments, Silver School is now supporting and enriching each day of the rest of the lives of those who are over the age of sixty-five. Most of all, we are implanting the hope and vision of the kingdom of God for these people. Most human beings will grow old. My heart's desire is that all Christians, not only our church, will approach the elderly with a gentle hand and a smile.

26 ⊕ EXPRESSION OF CARE THROUGH PRACTICAL SACRIFICE

How would you ruin a beautiful garden? You could burn it up or flood it out. An even easier way that doesn't take any work to accomplish is just to leave it alone. The weeds will soon take over, and the beautiful garden will be ruined. The same thing applies to human relationships, such as between a husband and wife. What could trigger a conflict between them? One could probably find faults, or slander, or openly criticize the weaknesses of the other. Yet those things are not necessary; all one needs to do is ignore the other.

How, then, would I go about ruining my own life? Ignoring and devaluing my soul as if there is no God is the shortcut to doing so. Concern for things that have life is essential. Being concerned is the way we respect and bring life to living things.

These days, especially with the apparent lack of compassion and generosity in the world, people desperately need someone who is genuinely concerned for them. Sincere concern doesn't stop with just a word but, rather, results in substantial devotion that requires sacrifice.

Our church understands this basic need and, with genuine concern, has made every effort to serve the elderly. One way we do this is by offering tour programs for the Silver School. Twice a year we plan a special tour outing and invite members and non-members alike to join. Currently there are between 200 and 250 elders who participate, with non-members comprising the greater portion. This large number of participants requires five or six tour buses to be reserved for the trip, and special care is needed when facing the challenges of feeding so large a group. A sizeable amount of time is spent in preparation and planning for these events. The cost of hosting tours is also something to consider, including bus rental fee, food, refreshments, and gifts among other things. Hosting tours twice a year is a financial burden on our church, but there are some individuals who sacrificially support this ministry with their finances and prayer.

In spite of the challenging factors, we continue with this ministry because the people need our concern desperately. They seldom have this kind of opportunity. Serving and sacrificing for the elderly shows that our church loves them and cares for them in practical ways. We would love for all of them who participate in the tours to join the Silver School, but we do not push them. We are pleased they can experience the love of Christ through our service, which puts the spotlight on those who are typically neglected in our society.

We are also seeking other ways to minister to them in the coming years. We are planning to equip the Silver School with more educational materials for them to utilize in small group settings. We are researching and developing more curricula. It is our hope, through the comprehensive ministry of the Silver School, to reach the elderly in more meaningful ways.

27 ⊕ RIGHTEOUS MINISTRY DECISIONS

American aviator Charles Lindbergh flew from New York to Paris in his single-engine airplane, *The Spirit of St. Louis*. The flight took thirty-three hours and thirty minutes. The historic, nonstop flight in a single-seat airplane elevated him to hero status in two countries. A large crowd gathered to celebrate his achievement as he landed.

There is a little-known backstory that goes along with this account. One of the guests at the landing, the CEO of a cigarette company, approached Charles and said, "I will give you $50,000 if you hold this cigarette in your hand."

But the reply he received was, "I am sorry, sir, but I am a Christian."

The CEO did not give up after the first refusal. He once again asked him to "just hold the cigarette in your mouth for a photo and receive $50,000."

Once again Charles said, "I am a baptized Christian," firmly declining the second offer. The next day this story was publicized in a newspaper in Paris. It moved many Christians in Paris to donate more than $100,000 to Charles Lindbergh.

Regardless of whether this anecdote is true, we see modeled in it a Christian value of dying to sin and living for Christ. He may have seemed too rigid to worldly people, yet he exemplified his Christianity and was not moved by unrighteousness. This story is a good lesson for us in how we should respond. We need to stick to biblical principles in whatever situations we are in.

After I had been ministering in Sangamdong Church for three years, we started to construct our own building. In the original design, the ground floor was to be approximately 5,247 square feet with 1,172 square feet of that space rented to a branch of the Korean Federation of Community Credit Cooperatives (KFCCC). One day we received a phone call from someone at a prestigious bank. He offered a large sum per square foot to rent 3,978 square feet on the ground floor beside the KFCCC. At that time, we were in debt by approximately $665,000 for the construction costs. What they were offering would amount to more than $2,000,000. With that amount of money we could pay off all our debts and still deposit more than $1,000,000 in the bank to accrue interest. This was a huge temptation to our church.

After much thought, I decided to refuse the offer for the simple reason that we had not constructed the building to make a profit on renting space. Of course, we had agreed in advance to rent a portion to KFCCC to reduce our financial burden, but we could not compromise our goals and use the whole first floor for commercial business because that did not fit with our mission. My choice may seem regrettable from a human perspective, and some may say it was unwise. My first thought was to rationalize accepting by focusing on the fact that it would get the church out of debt and give us extra money for our ministry. But then I remembered that the church was given to the Lord. I had to ask myself if it was right and righteous to modify the mission.

With a burden of $665,000 in debt, I was conflicted in the process of considering the offer. I knew what we needed was prayer. Prayer never fails to lead us to the right path in the simplest and most accurate way. I asked God if it was his will for us to give the whole first floor to renters, and I realized it was not what he wanted. Although several members were tempted, we were able to focus on what God wanted after the request went out on the prayer chain. We decided instead to open a nursery in that space to take care of the children in the community. This ministry was nothing compared to the profit we could have earned by renting to the bank, but it was part of the vision of the church that needed to be carried out.

This plan was not easy to pursue because the government at that time did not allow nurseries for religious institutions. They did, however, allow nurseries on property allocated for educational research. Because of all the new condominiums that were being constructed around Sangamdong Church, there were many young couples with nursery-aged children looking for a nursery school for them while they were at work. We felt helpless in our efforts to assist them. But once again God opened a door for us. Some people in the community who knew our vision informed us that the government had a policy that if renovation plans had not been finalized, one could apply to modify the stated use of a building. As a result, we modified the purpose of our ground floor to be an educational and research institution, which then allowed us to have the nursery school. It is my belief that God helped us overcome this obstacle as a reward for our financial sacrifice. Finally, Sangamdong Nursery School (SNS) was opened and now has a waiting list for applicants.

When we do our part, even though there is sometimes great sacrifice, God will take care of the rest. When you obey in the small things, you do not need to worry about anything. God, who received our obedience, took care of the problem for Sangamdong Church. God established the nursery in our church, and it has blessed us in more ways than we ever expected.

Do our churches obey and do what is needed? Facing the choices at hand, do I submit myself to God's leadership? Let us not forget that it is God who protects the church. Following God's will and not our own plans is how we obey, and allows him to protect the church.

28 ⊕ WE ARE GOD'S MASTERPIECES

The book *Temptation that Has Reasons*, written by Cheolje Cho, discusses a number of famous brands and what they represent: Chanel symbolizes French-upper-class fashion; Louis Vuitton created the legendary monogram canvas; Bulgari renovated women's fashion, emphasizing the uniqueness and activeness of women; and Christian Dior markets women's beauty the best, to name a few. The author justifies that the fame of these luxury brands have their own ground. He explains that these masterpieces have been created through long effort, through craftsmanship that seeks the best quality, and through pure, sacrificial service to customers. Those top brands were not born that way, he notes.

A similar principle can be applied to us. The apostle Paul confessed that we are all sinners. But God created us as his masterpieces. God designed his creation to be the best quality, to be shaped and molded with time. Just as the value of the top brand names was not acquired in one day, we need to live our lives the best we can so our lives will be recognized and influential among others because we are the masterpiece of God's creation. While we live lives worthy of a masterpiece, we must also look at others as the masterpieces they are. This concept is true in ministry as well. Our church's nursery capacity is only for eighty-four children, but we have a long waiting list that, at one time, had one thousand children on it. Perhaps the long list is a result of our education philosophy, in which we look at each, individual child as a masterpiece of God.

We pay special attention to the food we provide for these young children. A lot of parents want to know what kind of food their children will receive at nursery school. We try to exceed their expectations. We never lower our food budget to save money. I always emphasize the following: First, we do not purchase frozen meat. Second, we only use quality oil—for example, grape seed oil or olive oil. Third, we do our best to choose the freshest vegetables; sometimes they are donated by church members who have gardens. Last, we provide highly nutritious snacks, such as corn, potatoes, and sweet potatoes rather than pizza or hamburgers. The cost for our endeavor is somewhat higher as a result, but we value the health of the children more than our budget. Our effort assures the health of our children and the trust of the parents. Our parents understand how carefully we choose the highest-quality ingredients for their children, and they spread the word to their neighbors, which also shines a positive light on the image of our church in the community. On the other hand, our effort also results in deficits in the nursery's finances, so the church must find ways to support the nursery every month.

I have great respect for the nursery staff, who are faithful in fulfilling their mission for the church through the children. We give extra care to the nursery because we look at and value each child through the eyes of God, who created them as his masterpieces. We want to teach the children and their parents to understand who they really are in God's sight. Our unique educational philosophy and love for them have led us to pay attention to the smallest details. It is important to take action, starting with the small things. Even when these things seem to create a hardship at first, we know they will eventually lead us and the church to live as masterpieces.

29 ⊕ DISABILITY MINISTRY: SNTC

People from all over Seoul visit Sangamdong's stunning parks, especially on the weekends and holidays. When the weather is especially nice, the streets are lined with parked cars, and people are fully enjoying the beautiful parks. In the fall, people gather at Sky Park for the Miscanthus Festival. And in the spring, yellow forsythia bushes adorn the park, waving gracefully in the wind. Using this beautiful park as a backdrop, many people take photos or have picnic lunches, enjoying the breathtaking beauty of the season. Many who come to the park break off branches of the forsythia to take home with them. The staff at the park do not even try to stop this behavior because they know that this type of pruning will ultimately be good for the bushes as they grow fuller and more beautiful.

Do you ever feel like you are the ugly, broken branch? You needn't worry; God can take the difficult situation and bring about new life, just like the pruning of the branch of the flowering bush. Going through difficulty in life produces more fruit. Trust the Lord, who will lead you through the changes, and depend on him in the difficult situations in your life and also in the ministry of the church.

Sangamdong Church experienced this kind of transformative change in the form of our Sangamdong Nazarene Therapy Center (SNTC). Just as adults speaking to children may kneel down to get on their level in order to show consideration for them, it is the job of the church to show consideration for others by trying to see things from another point of view. Sometimes it requires us to give up our advantage, or our pride. To have consideration for others, we must find a place in our mind where we can see things from the other person's perspective. We need to keep in mind that Jesus, who came down from heaven in human form, was the ultimate model in considering others. Based on his life, we need to put forth the effort to do the same every day.

There are people groups who need our special concern, and one of those groups is comprised of disabled people. As people who have experienced the love of Jesus—who was the best care-giver—the church has an obligation to this people group, and we also have the capacity to embrace and take care of them. As a way of showing our care and love for them, we launched SNTC on the fourth floor of the church. We are very proud of this facility. The students are disabled children to whom we provide speech, art, music, and play therapies. My dream is that this space would present freedom to these special children who come to learn, get therapy, and play.

The reason I have such an interest in this ministry is that one of our church members, Soojin Kim, was teaching in the speech therapy department at KNU, and she was especially concerned for the disabled children. She wanted to help the parents of autis-tic children who usually have speech disabilities. She committed her life to caring for these children, especially in the area of her specialty, speech therapy, which is typically associated with chil-dren. Professor Kim volunteered to help autistic children improve their speech at our facility, SNTC. Through this ministry, I real-ized that God had fulfilled my dream and sent me the right per-son. If it had just been up to me to plan and cast a vision, things would not be flowing as smoothly. God knew my heart and vision and led the right servant, who is devoted to equipping disabled children, enabling us to fulfill this important part of his ministry.

After starting with just one person, we now have other sup-port staff from the KNU speech therapy department. I am amazed by and so thankful for all of this help. We currently have ninety children who regularly visit our facility for therapy. It may not be usual for a church to run this type of center for budgetary or resource reasons. But we are showing the love of God through our consideration for the disabled. Our prayer is that God would give us wisdom to know and be aware of the real needs. SNTC was established not from our heart or wisdom but by God's direction.

Although at the start of the ministry we had big, God-led visions, we still experienced several difficult situations. The life of a child with a disability can be difficult, yet in some ways it can be even more difficult on the parents raising that child. It is not easy for someone who has not personally dealt with the issues to understand the suffering parents experience. Dealing with the negative attitudes of others and poor educational environments for their children can leave them frustrated and exhausted, but their love for their children motivates them to carry on.

With this understanding, we had to embrace the parents along with the children in our pursuit of the SNTC ministry. And this was not an easy task. We have never tried to make a profit with this ministry, and we do not pressure the families to join or even attend our church. Of course, our ultimate goal is to win their souls by divine touch through lifestyle evangelism, but we never ask anything of them in exchange for what we are doing for them. We simply serve them with the love of Christ in all areas.

SNTC has been in operation since 2003, but there has not yet been one convert and, amazingly, not even one new member added to our church from those whom this ministry serves. Some may wonder why we even still operate SNTC. Some of our church members have the same question! Others ask about reducing the space used for SNTC so we can utilize the space for the church. I appreciate that these voicing their thoughts are doing so out of love for the church; however, SNTC is an important part of the essence and mission of our church. There is more to the mission than just the instantly visible benefits. We are called to care for the marginalized people groups in our society. This is why we have befriended them and not stopped our mission of serving them over the past several years. And we will continue in the coming years to share the love of God with them.

We need to remember that God is in charge of the financial situation. Our calculations are not the same as his. Our part is to do the best to fulfill the mission we have been given. We need not depend on our calculations but embrace the children and their parents with unconditional love.

The difficulties we have had with the SNTC have been nothing more than the temporary pain of pruning the forsythia branches. We will witness increased flowers as a result of the broken branches. Yes, we still struggle with the financial deficit, but we have earned the reputation of having the best teachers, and there is a waiting list of applicants. We are now dreaming bigger. We will not cease to dream. We hope to enlarge the facility's capabilities to develop even more therapy programs—for instance, for mothers who take care of special-needs children day in and day out by themselves. We would like to have a daycare center. Though we do not have space for one yet, we believe God will provide in his timing.

30 ⊕ WHEN YOU GIVE, GIVE ALL

There is a story of three brothers who went on an adventure to find strange treasures. When they finally came back from their journey, the oldest had found an unusual telescope that let him see things in other places. The second one had found a flying carpet, and the youngest had found an apple that could cure any disease. One day, the oldest brother was looking through his telescope, and he saw a princess dying in a faraway land. The king, looking for someone to cure his daughter, announced that the man who saved her life would be allowed to marry her. Upon telling his brother this, all three brothers got on the flying carpet of the second brother and flew to that kingdom. The youngest brother gave the magic apple to the princess, and when she bit into the apple, she was cured. Then the three brothers began to argue about who would marry the princess since they all had contributed to help save her life. The king pondered it and made the decision that the youngest should marry her. His reason was that the other brothers still possessed their treasures, but the youngest brother had given up his treasure and had nothing left.

Only having one thing, and giving that one thing, is to give all—our hearts. Among all the different ministries in our church that the members are committed to, there is one with which all of them faithfully help each year. We started it in the year 2000, and as part of our lifestyle-evangelism campaign, we call it the Loving and Sharing with Our Neighbors Bazaar. The Saturday before Harvest Moon Day—called Thanksgiving in Korea—we have a bazaar where we share the abundant fruits of the harvest with the less fortunate in our community who do not have families to spend the holiday with. We started out inviting just our church members, but for the past several years, we have opened the doors and extended the love to the neighborhood. Our bazaar has become the largest in the Sangamdong area and is known as a community festival in the neighborhood. It was even recognized by Mapo District, where Sangamdong is located, and received awards in 2008 and 2009, and was also prized as the best social welfare event of the year by the Seoul Social Welfare Association in 2010.

For this bazaar, we as a church spend quite a bit of time in research. We have seen other churches try to put on bazaars, but they have not appeared to have the outcome we were looking for. In reviewing why, I found that part of the reason may be due to the fact that they bring in outside merchants to sell their goods, and in turn those merchants give a portion of their sales to the church. Many bazaars are operated that way, and this is where we differ. Our bazaar is more like a community festival in traditional Korean style. Church members volunteer to cook all kinds of well-loved Korean festival-type foods—drinks and desserts that are not easy to make and not often made in homes these days. All sorts of pancakes, grain juices, kimchi, and rice cakes are made and sold. One year, the traffic officers had to come and help manage the gathering crowds and vehicles.

We are not so concerned with the size but, rather, the quality of the items we provide to our neighbors at a low price. For instance, making kimchi requires carefully selecting the freshest ingredients, including chili powder and special other spices to give that unique kimchi taste. The older ladies of the congregation know all the secrets from their mothers. They do not buy ready-made kimchi from the market but go to the fields to buy the chilies, sun-dry them on the top floor of the church, and then take the best care of them until they are finally ground. The Chinese cabbages are also specifically purchased by the church elders from the surrounding farms or the farming association to ensure the highest quality. Kimchi—made with 100% domestically grown ingredients and prepared to taste like Mother's—is not something that is easily obtainable these days. We do give a slight priority to church members before opening up sales to the community. Aside from kimchi, we also make specially seasoned soy sauces, boiling to perfection apples, lemons, onions, and other vegetables. Because the housewives from the neighborhood prepare these items with their own hands, word-of-mouth advertisement for our bazaar spreads easily. All the ingredients for our food items are guaranteed to be the highest quality—especially for the snacks for children.

As we prepare for the event, we are undeniably physically exhausted, but at the same time, we are willing to sacrifice and provide good things to our neighborhood. Our goal is to give our best and our all. As a result, we routinely raise upwards of $20,000 each year we hold the bazaar, even in the year 2011, when we had unexpectedly heavy rains. We donate our annual net profit from this event to the Mapo District Community Center and Welfare Association, and we thank the Lord for it all.

Through our efforts, the church has earned the trust of our community, and our church members have built relationships and learned the happiness of being one in heart. They have experienced great joy by giving all they had and by reaching their goal together. The thing for which we are most thankful is that we have seen the fruit of our evangelism efforts in the community. I hope this event will continue every year. And I hope that those who have received will also learn the joy of giving to others so our efforts will extend from our community to our country and beyond.

31 ⊕ CHURCH IS A SANCTUARY WITH KINDNESS AND TRUST

Recently one of our church members who works at a bakery came to me complaining about some unpleasant customers. She explained that sometimes she has a hard time understanding how some customers could be untruthful. One customer came to the bakery with a half-eaten loaf of bread and tried to convince her that the bread was old and requested a fresh loaf at no cost. Another customer loudly argued that he had found something inside his bread, but he did not bring in the evidence to prove it; he simply thrust it at her, demanding she exchange it with a freshly baked loaf or refund his money. She admitted that she nearly lost her temper and was about to respond in the same way.

I totally understand how frustrated she felt in that kind of situation because I felt frustrated just listening to her. There are so many times in our lives when we need to be patient. If she had responded to the customer impatiently, she may have felt better in the moment, but she would probably lose that customer for good. Although I sympathized with how she felt, I advised her to be kind and patient even with those types of people.

It is imperative that we remember that kindness is the foundation of building a relationship on trust. Insincere kindness can be sensed immediately, but consistent kindness plants the seeds of trust. When people comment that this is a good bakery, or a good hospital, or even a good church, the implication is that its people are kind and trustworthy. Maintaining one's composure, even in the most unreasonable and frustrating situations, will successfully build the trust that is not easy to obtain and surely bring about a difference in society. Sacrifice and patience are vital in earning that trust.

The first time our church donated our total net income from the bazaar to the district government offices, it was a controversial decision that not everyone agreed with. There were many different ideas of how to use the income from the bazaar. Some members hesitated to give all of it and instead suggested a partial donation, considering all the time and effort that went into preparing for the bazaar. Others suggested we just help those in need ourselves, without going through the hands of the government, so that our church would get the recognition. I felt that our sharing the profits should be anonymous because we are not seeking praise. So I set up the annual donation officially between the community center and the government office so we wouldn't have to repeat the argument from year to year. By overcoming this conflict in the church and giving all our profits, we earned the trust of the neighbors and shared kindness with them. Organizations that have successful bazaars are often questioned about how they are using the income. In our church, however, the members were guaranteed financial transparency because they witnessed that we sacrificed in giving all we made.

If we had decided to use some of the money for the church to reduce the conflict within the church, things would probably be different now. The conflict might have been reduced, but the trust between the church and community might not be in the place it is now. Through the bazaar, our church members truly experience how to serve and give to others. Because we started out not compromising and giving all when the income was not much in the beginning, they give even more now without hesitation. We as a church decided to give the whole, not just a part, and we gave from our hearts, not out of obligation.

Through our efforts, our church has received strong support from the community, and we have naturally experienced church growth from that. Those in the community perceived Sangam-dong Church as a small church that gave all. Not only with the bazaar, but in every activity with which our church is involved, we strive to show our integrity to the community. We have endured some internal conflicts, but our congregation is now more active in the various community services, which spreads our reputation as a kind and trustworthy church. There is no denying that we now live in an era where people think that even churches cannot be trusted. We want to prove that the church is the one place in this world where they can trust and find kindness. My hope is that the love of God would reach these people through our commitment and that the clear image of our church implanted in our neighborhood would reflect the love of God.

32 ⊕ GIVING IMMEDIATE HELP

Many of us have a tendency to be quick to say things but slow to do them. Often we fail to act even when we want or intend to. We easily promise to find time to get together with friends, but how often do we actually take the time to be with them? How many times have we felt guilty over not having taken the time needed and now our friend is in trouble?

Koreans have a saying that God has given us three gifts of gold, or *geum*: The first is the gift of pure gold, or *hwang-geum*, which makes us rich. The second is the gift of salt, or *so-geum*, which gives flavor to our food. The last is the gift of now, or *ji-ge-um*, which means the present moment. Look at the people around you. Jesus said, "What good will it be for someone to gain the whole world, yet forfeit their soul? Or what can anyone give in exchange for their soul?" (Matthew 16:26). There are so many souls that need our love and care right in our own neighborhoods.

What are ways that we can help those who need help *now*? Many times, we are not physically able to do what our hearts desire. We are often dealing with our own immediate needs and cannot help others. In any case, the church can be the answer. The church is always open; anyone can enter if they need. The church is ready to embrace those who need help now and help them at the present moment. The building itself does not qualify the church to do this job. Rather, it is the people who are ready to welcome the suffering.

With this in mind, we have tried several different things. First, we offered legal consultations free of charge. Many people are perplexed when they have to deal with legal issues. Unless they happen to know a lawyer, they will probably do without because of the considerable cost of legal help. To help meet the needs of the people, our church provided free legal consultation services.

Several church members volunteered as a team under the leadership of a lawyer and made this service available to everyone. Since there is no financial burden to use the service, some inquire about urgent matters, and some come with general legal questions.

Another area we offered was free service for health consultations. One of the members of our church is a doctor who volunteered to assist with this service. People came with general concerns regarding their health, not those suffering from serious illnesses. He gave general checkups and referred them to specialists for follow-up when appropriate. He also gave advice for living healthy lifestyles, with specific focus on people's physical abilities. Every one of us is concerned with our physical health, so it is helpful to have a health consultation when needed. But many in our community are not able to see a doctor or get medical help in a clinic, so our church found a way to help these people. The medical and legal services were basically run by volunteers.

Additionally, every Tuesday a doctor came to the Silver School to give acupuncture and foot massage therapy to the elderly. A foot massage training course was offered to volunteer church members on Wednesdays, and they now serve the elderly both inside and outside the church. Through this type of service, we are able to give immediate help to our neighbors, and people now recognize our church as healthy. They understand that our service is not built around making a profit but out of a pure heart with a servant attitude.

Churches can share the love of God even without any professional volunteers' help, but if professional volunteers are available it is good, knowing "that in all things God works for the good of those who love him, who have been called according to his purpose" (Romans 8:28). Anyone who is a devoted worker can use their gifts in serving the church according to God's purpose, even if they are not medical doctors or lawyers.

Unfortunately, we have had to suspend our legal and health consultations for the time being. Since they were free, many people received the help they needed, but there were also a few who abused the system. We have not given up, but we are trying to find a more effective way. I recommend churches take the time to research and find a model that will fit within their contexts. I myself will continue to find ways to give immediate help to those who are in need.

Do you have some souls in need who come to your mind right now? Do not pass up the opportunity to go to them in Christian love. The church should be the first to do this!

33 ⊕ HELPING TO SOLVE HEART ISSUES

Recently we have seen a consistent increase in the number of suicides among celebrities in Korea. Korea has the highest suicide rate of the countries in the Organization for Economic Cooperation and Development (OECD). Why is the suicide rate so high in this country? And why does the suicide atmosphere spread from an individual level to a social level? One possible reason could be that many people are overwhelmed by the present economic situation. Some people choose suicide when they feel absolutely helpless as a result of their overwhelming financial problems. What is even sadder is that people begin to sympathize with those who have died this way, saying it was the terrible economic situation that drove them to their deaths. This thinking may be one of the factors causing the increase in our society.

But the fact is, there are many people in bad financial situations who are able to overcome and find true happiness in life. How, then, can we say that suicide is caused by the situation in which one finds oneself? There is another factor that cannot be denied, and that is the condition of the heart. There are many people who are tempted to commit suicide because they think they would rather die than face certain situations in their lives. But there are also those who have overcome the temptation and are living their lives instead.

Statistics reveal that many who succumb to suicide suffer from severe depression, autism, lack of affection, and many other, related issues. What this means is that people are hurting, and their hearts are broken. How can people overcome the crises in their lives that are caused by the problems of the heart? Christians can help them. Of course, even Christians experience problems of the heart, but we have a clear answer to solving those problems. In all circumstances, we know that we can overcome by holding on to the Holy Spirit. The church, with the help of our source of healing—namely, the Holy Spirit—should first deal with our own problems of the heart and then go out and help our neighbors to solve their heart problems.

For those dealing with this contemporary issue of wounded hearts, especially those suffering from clinical depression, our church is now taking action. As our church grows, we have been able to make more attempts to meet the needs in our society. Our first attempt has been the worship service targeting office workers. In Korea, the office workers are mainly men, and they usually have a very routine day. As the head of the family, they must work very hard to make a living to support the family, which leaves their hearts dry and poor. We are excited about this special ministry that prioritizes helping them. On Wednesdays at noon, we have a worship service for those who work near our church. We currently have between twenty and thirty regulars who gather to worship. Our church also provides lunch for them after the service. Our vision is to help them initiate a Christian fellowship in each workplace. We are exploring ways for them to gather and worship right in their own offices on a regular basis.

In 2002, Sangamdong was designated as a future digital-media city (DMC) in the new Seoul City plan, and more than 140 acres of land around our church is beginning to be occupied by various cultural enterprises and media corporations. Among those are the top Korean broadcast companies, such as KBS, MBC, SBS, YNT, TBS, and more. The digital-media city is now approaching completion, and we are expecting that our church will be surrounded by many celebrities, news outlets, broadcast studios, and various other entertainment companies. In light of this expectation, our church has planned a special ministry of counseling for celebrities. Although their lives are continually highlighted by the media and they are adored by the public, they often feel alone in their off-camera lives—more than we can even imagine. Among celebrities who have recently shocked many with a series of suicide attempts have been quite a number of Christians. They were simply not able to overcome their pain even though they had once come to know God. They were not able to overcome the crises in their lives because they failed to maintain a healthy relationship with the Lord and allow the Holy Spirit to lead them. There is no question that our ministry will be able to help both Christians and non-Christians alike to meet the Lord and grow in him. It is for this reason that our church is prepared for this new ministry to celebrities. Since these people are working in the public eye, they can eventually share the gospel more effectively as they are transformed by the true Spirit. We hope to see the transformation of these people by fulfilling our mission.

We hope this will not be solely a ministry of our church but that other churches in Sangamdong would join with us and lead people to the Lord. We know the church is the place to find the most powerful key to solving the problems of the heart.

34 ⊕ PASSION: CRISIS TURNS INTO OPPORTUNITY

Yongmo Cho, the author of a recent best-seller in Korea, *Proposing a Million Times*, studied in a rural area until he went to Seoul for his high school education. He studied hard and graduated from both Seoul National University and graduate school, majoring in law. He passed the government exams and began working in a government office. At the young age of twenty-seven, he became disabled in a most unfortunate hit-and-run accident that totally changed his life.

As a result of his anger, frustration, self-denial and devastation, he attempted to commit suicide. However, after he was unsuccessful, he began to realize his life was worth something. He understood that it would not be easy to find a job with his disability. He was finally hired by an insurance company after the submission of his 110th job application, and he began his second life as a life planner. He was passionate about his job and never lost a customer, no matter how cranky they were. He continually put his customers first and did his best to help each one and, as a result, was named Life Planner of the Year for his company.

"What is important is not how capable I am but how I use my abilities," stated Mr. Cho. He treats each moment in life as if it were an eternity by pouring all his passion into living and doing his best to make the most of every moment.

We should approach our ministries the way Mr. Cho approaches his life. There may be times in church ministry when it feels as if we are experiencing a moment of crisis, but I am sure that in the eyes of God there are no moments of crisis. When we give our best to God, he will lead us to bear the precious fruit.

When I first came to Sangamdong Church, the city was full of construction sites preparing stadiums for the 2002 World Cup games. Many houses and buildings were demolished to make room, and the people were moved out of town, including our church members. As many members moved away, our church seemed to empty as well. I felt tense and frustrated, thinking that the church just might have to close.

Before long, keeping my eyes on the Lord, I started to evangelize on the street. The final stop for Public Bus #5 was the present-day Sangamdong Rotary, which was my target mission field. This is now a familiar street with many restaurants and buildings, but it was just a dusty street at that time. On the corner sat a small grocery store where the items on the shelves were covered in a layer of dust from the nearby construction sites. The dust was so bad that we often saw street sweepers cleaning the dusty roads. This scenario is hard to imagine now, but this is what Sangam-dong was like in 2002.

I struggled in many ways because I did not have any experience in this type of evangelism. The month was June, and summer had come. I folded the sleeves of my shirt twice, wore a brightly colored necktie, and held my Bible in one hand. Folding my sleeves twice was a tip I had received from a leadership training. We were told that men looked energized and hardworking when they wore a white dress shirt with a brightly colored tie and their sleeves folded twice.

I was uneasy about stopping a passerby to share the gospel. I knew I must make every effort in the given situation. One day, I saw some children walking down the street whom I recognized as ones who already attended our Sunday school. Although I did not need to invite them to church and introduce the gospel to them, I still wanted to do something for them, so I decided to treat them with some snacks from the corner store. I bought some goodies, and the clerk put them in a black plastic bag. The bag full of snacks only cost me about $2.00 at that time. I started doing this for the children on a regular basis.

Children are always excited when they get a gift bag, and they want to share that excitement with their parents. These children were no exception. They showed their parents, who wondered how they kept getting bags of snacks on the street. At first, some of them confessed to me later, they were worried that the children may have taken them from the store. But they were relieved and a bit surprised when their children proudly told them that the new pastor from the church had given them the goodies.

Although this was just a small treat for the children, the parents were impressed. Because they felt that the pastor cared for their children, they encouraged their kids to attend Sunday school, and some of the parents even joined our worship service as a result.

I have never stopped presenting goodie bags to the children. They love me and always run to greet me every time they see me on the street, and the store lady loves me too! She thanked me because I was refreshing their stock that otherwise ended up dusty on the shelves. And she began to tell her other customers about me, saying that the new young pastor lovingly treated the children with goodie bags all the time. She shared about me so much that other young mothers in the community also started to come to our church. We now call this #5 Bus Stop Evangelism, and recognize that this helped establish the foundation of our children's church. I wonder sometimes how different things would be if I had just thought the situation was hopeless and had not made the effort to evangelize on the street. I am thankful God enabled me to stay focused; even when I found it difficult to stop people passing by to talk with them, God sustained the ministry in that environment.

Even now, I do not take any moment for granted, especially when it comes to saving souls—whether it is sharing the gospel with a person passing by on a dusty street, or any challenging situation in which I find myself. God remembers the passion of the minister who did his best in the moment. He will reward us with the blessings of everlasting fruit. And he will walk with us in the midst of the most difficult and challenging circumstances.

35 ⊕ THE MOST PRECIOUS BEING

A professor pulled a hundred-dollar bill from his pocket and showed the students in the middle of a lecture. He asked for anyone who wanted this nice, new, hundred-dollar bill to raise their hands. Of course, most of the students raised their hands. He then said he would like to give it to one of them, but then he crumpled it up and asked if they still wanted it. Again they raised their hands. Next, he threw it on the ground and stomped on it and asked if they still wanted it. No matter how the money was treated, its value never changed, and people still wanted it.

On this journey called life, we often fall, get trampled, and become dirty. The pain of failure and backsliding remains in our hearts. Some who suffer from those pains may feel they are useless. But no matter how terribly our lives has been stained, or how we have failed, there is an unchanging truth about us: We are the children of God—whom he bought with the blood of Jesus Christ.

The mission of the church is to let others know they are highly valued by God. Living in this era when people are evaluated by their achievements, successes and careers, many people have low self-esteem. The church has a responsibility to convince them that they are loved just as they are by the God who created them.

At Christmastime, our church goes from house to house singing Christmas carols in the early morning, following the tradition of the shepherds who glorified and praised God at the birth of the Christ child at the manger. Korean churches visit neighboring houses in the community as well as the homes of church members. This beautiful tradition has almost disappeared because people don't want to be awakened from their sleep these days. Sadly, urban people treat the beautiful melody of the Christmas songs as some kind of noise pollution.

Our church, however, in the middle of Seoul, has kept the tradition for the past fifty-eight years. With layers of thick coats and earmuffs, our members visit the neighbors and share the joy of Christmas Day. When the temperature is extremely cold, you will find them arm in arm to keep each other warm as they travel together to share their stories and testimonies. I remember one year, one of the older ladies suggested that we share things for which we are thankful. An elderly gentleman in his seventies confessed that the best gift he had ever received was when he met Jesus Christ and received him into his heart. A youth then gave a testimony that he was able to overcome the pain of a breakup with his girlfriend and, through prayer, had become closer to the Lord. Another member was thankful his children were finally able to find work by the grace of God. All the carolers shared about the love and grace of God with each other and the neighbors.

While caroling we receive many gifts, especially from church members. When people are blessed by our songs, they want to share something with us. These gifts gave us an idea about a new ministry we could use to bless other, smaller churches that were not able to be self-supporting. We receive a large amount of gifts; some give food items such as fruit or snacks, and others give clothes, toys, or daily necessities and other items. None of these gifts are used by our own church. Instead, we put them in large boxes and send them to between ten and fifteen churches we have previously recognized as being in need.

One church in the countryside shared their testimony with us, which was an encouragement for our ministry. They shared they did not have enough budget to provide children with refreshments after Sunday school, and they had noticed that children were slowly leaving to attend larger churches nearby. The church was so thankful because the food from this new ministry enabled them to feed the children for more than six months. This church's testimony was a precious reminder for us as we shared about the birth of our Lord.

Sadly, worldly things—such as drinking and other entertainment on Christmas Day—are taking the place of the One Christmas is all about. But we still have a chance to fulfill our mission.

We must let others know of the holy sacrifice and love of Jesus Christ, who came to save us, and let them know of his love toward each one of us with no exceptions. In whatever situation we are, even at the lowest point in our lives, we are still important to the Lord. Because of this mission, our church keeps the tradition of Christmas caroling. With prayerful hearts, we praise and share the blessings from our Lord with our neighbors. Of course, it is not only on Christmas Day that we should show love but every day. We do not want to miss any opportunity to have an impact on our neighbors.

36 ⊕ GIVE THANKS WITH THE HEART OF A DEBTOR

Do you know how much it costs to implant a single strand of hair? In my country, the cost is about ten dollars. This may sound like a reasonable price—but who would want to implant a single strand? If you want visible volume, you would need at least several thousand strands, and the cost then goes up. One hundred strands would cost one thousand dollars, and one thousand strands would be ten thousand dollars. Even so, they say that one thousand strands do not make much of a difference since most people have around two hundred thousand strands of hair, so one thousand strands would not even fill in one small area. Based on these numbers, a full head of hear would cost about two million dollars. So does this mean that those who have a lot of hair are actually millionaires?

Thanksgiving is a mindset. When we change our mindset, we are able to be thankful for everything. I personally have an endless list of things to thank the Lord for since coming to Sangam-dong Church. I thank the Lord that he placed the church here. I thank the Lord that the neighbors met him in our church and in turn shared the gospel with their neighbors, who have all devoted themselves to the church. Moreover, I am amazed by the grace of God in how he revived the church and has enabled us to fulfill our mission—neither of which occurred through our own ability. Just as those who have a full head of hair forget to be thankful for it, we too may forget to give thanks for all the blessings we receive from God.

When we become aware of the blessings, what should we do? Express our heartfelt thanks to the Lord in words alone? True confession does not end with thanksgiving; it requires action. If you were given a needed organ and the funds to pay for the surgery, would you simply say thank you? You would probably want to *show* how thankful you are by *doing* something. You would live with the heart of someone who owes a great debt to the donor of that organ for the rest of your life.

Our church owes a debt; we have received abundant blessings from the Lord, which are more incredible than what the donation of an internal organ would be. Our hearts are thankful, and to express our heartfelt thanks, we are sharing the blessings with our neighbors.

Our first support ministry began in 2003 to help churches who are not able to be self-supporting, which reminds us of our early days at Sangamdong Church. In this ministry I am reminded of the various people who have prayed and lent a hand to sustain me as a pastor up to this time. Our church has not forgotten the sacrificial giving from the American Nazarene churches and individuals who helped establish Sangamdong Church. We also remember the numerous church members who were committed to give to help build the new sanctuary, and most of all, we keep in mind the grace of God that has been leading us in all of our ministries.

The supporting ministry has been growing since it first began in 2003. We now help support forty-five different churches and organizations monthly. This fact itself is a great blessing that motivates us to be thankful and to share even more. We cannot be content with this support ministry, thinking we are paying back our debt to the Lord. We are doing a great ministry, but at the same time we are becoming more in debt to the Lord because it is not through our own efforts but by God's grace that our church has a budget sufficient to support other churches.

The Bible tells us, "Let no debt remain outstanding, except the continuing debt to love one another" (Romans 13:8). We have a great debt of love, so we will maintain this thankful heart and not take for granted the blessings from the Lord. We will keep giving thanks for the small and great blessings. We will do our best to repay our debt to the Lord by sharing what we have with others. We will not be proud or lax in our efforts and will always be thankful as we give back to the Lord.

37 ⊕ EFFECTIVE MINISTRY

There is a story of the young Andrew Carnegie visiting a success-ful businessman. On his office wall was a painting of a boat with an oar on a sandy beach. The boat was old and leaned heavily on its side; the whole painting communicated an atmosphere of gloom and hopelessness. At the bottom was the caption "The high tide will surely come."

Carnegie asked the businessman why he had this dark paint-ing hanging on the wall, and the businessman replied, "When I was a salesman, my life was once terribly miserable. It seemed hopeless, and I seemed helpless, which drove me to despair. One day I visited my mentor and saw a painting with these words. As a twenty-eight-year-old salesman, I believed the high tide would come to my life as well. The painting changed my despair into hope and became a great encouragement for my success."

This idea is applicable to Christians as well. Christians will encounter a high tide in their lives for sure. Even though the situ-ation may seem desperate and miserable for a time, and there may even be a dark tunnel to go through, we should dream and be ready for the days outside the tunnel to fulfill our job.

Sangamdong Church went through a dark time. From a hu-man perspective, it was full of darkness and despair, and we felt like we would not be able to fulfill our mission. Yet God allowed the high tide to flow to us. This high tide can flow to anyone or any church. God has a plan for each of us in his timing. Some-times he works it out himself, and other times he uses his people. God in his graciousness has not only brought the high tide to our church but has also enabled us to be his workers. He has allowed us to experience the high tide ourselves and also to facilitate a high tide for others so they can experience this amazing turning point. One thing God has given us to prepare for this mission is a passion for evangelism for our nation. The church is called to be missional. A church will become meaningless if it is not interested in sharing the gospel and saving souls. The church should be actively practicing various types of evangelism.

As the Korean churches grew, they began to focus on foreign missions. Many churches were committed to building churches in Southeast Asian countries, Japan, China, African countries, North European countries, Israel, and even in America, which had been our big brother in missions. They dispersed missionaries all over the globe, which was a challenging model for other churches in the world.

As foreign missions spread and grew, we saw the domestic churches becoming more and more empty. This seemed to be a negative effect of our missional effectiveness. Of course, when we speak of effectiveness, we do not do so from a human perspective. Strategically withdrawing the offerings for foreign missions is not an option. Yet the church should consider carefully the reason they are doing a particular ministry and research positive models and effectiveness. Through fervent prayer and faithful studies, a church should learn what God is asking them to do, and this will bring about missional effectiveness for the church.

Although foreign missions are important, we must balance the missional focus between foreign and domestic ministries. We cannot concentrate only on foreign missions while the national church is not being taken care of. The mission will be most effective when we really understand what the priorities are in the eyes of God—when, for whom, for what, and how God wants us to step out.

Our church sought to know the will of God for our ministry, and we learned that God was opening doors for us to support our national churches along with the foreign missionaries. This mission principle has been consistent ever since.

We will keep seeking what God wants us to sacrifice for the churches in our country. To know the heart of God, we will commit ourselves to prayer. We will also dream, under the leadership of the Lord, of the day when the high tide will come to every church in Korea. I also pray that every church in Korea will encounter another high-tide revival like we experienced in the early days. The spiritual high tide in the church is not just physical or numerical growth. It is spiritual revival where the high tide reaches our lonely boat. As a church, we are committed to come before our Lord with the same heart to remember and be thankful for the spiritual blessings that were once poured out upon our church.

38 ⊕ A VISION FOR REMOTE AREAS

The New Economics Foundation in England studied the Happy Planet Index (HPI) by countries. Korea came out in the middle among other countries, while the top-ranked countries were, in order from #1, Vanuatu, Colombia, and Costa Rica. Many of the higher-ranking countries in South America were, surprisingly, the meek ones, and countries like Bangladesh, which is so-called underdeveloped, ranked high among the Asian countries. This result explains that the happiness of a country's people is not proportional to its economic growth.

How are we now? Are you happy? If so, what is the standard you use to measure happiness? Is it wealth, honor, authority, or influential power? Do we not use these as values and the measuring standard for happiness? These are definitely all relatively configured, and relative values cannot bring us true happiness that never changes. We need to focus on what God has placed in our hands, even if those things seem small and insignificant. Happiness comes from being thankful. We can thank God for giving us a loving family, a place to work (even though work can make us physically tired at times), healthy bodies, and a new day each day with a new breath of fresh air.

Once upon a time, two friends who lived far away from each other set a date to meet at a specific location that was halfway between them. Each of them had to travel several days and nights by horseback over some rough trails, but they both finally arrived at the meeting point.

One man exclaimed to his friend and shared the story of what had happened to him on the way. He told how his horse had stepped on something sharp that had caused him to slip from the saddle and roll onto the ground. He feared he would break his leg in the fall, but when it was over, he realized he was unhurt. He immediately knelt on the ground and gave thanks to the Lord for keeping him safe.

The other friend was amazed at the story and told his friend about his own journey. He had an even more miraculous story because he had arrived without any accidents. He realized then how gracious the Lord had been to him in keeping him safe.

Which friend had the most to thank the Lord for? The one who fell from the saddle uninjured or the one who was spared any accidents on the journey? When we do not have any difficulties, we tend to take things for granted. Many times we do not realize what is truly precious in our lives until after we have passed through hardship and become aware of the protection of the Lord's hand on our lives. Many times we do not even realize it is the work of the Holy Spirit in our lives that prompts us to be thankful for the seemingly ordinary, simple things in our lives.

By the grace of God, I had the opportunity to become aware of something I had always taken for granted, and I learned an important lesson from it. During the traditional holiday times in my early years at Sangamdong Church, I noticed a fluctuation in attendance. As the church grew larger, I was surprised that attendance began to decrease during the holidays. Later I learned that many members leave the city for their hometown to visit parents during those times.

I learned a significant lesson through this experience, which was that urban church growth is not simply from our efforts and is not just God showing favor to us. There are churches in rural areas that have sustained the Christian faith for generations, and people then move from there to the cities for various reasons. Conservatively speaking, about one-third of urban church members come from rural churches, where they met Jesus Christ and grew spiritually. One could say that those rural churches planted the present urban churches.

The statistics for our church membership show that quite a number of our members were Christians before they started coming to our church. I am embarrassed to say that various rural and smaller churches did all the evangelizing and Christian education for many in my congregation. God has helped us see that we need to be thankful for these churches that carry out an important mission. And he has given us a vision for these churches.

In the previous chapters I mentioned that God has given us a vision for national evangelism, and with this mission, we are focused even more on revival of the rural churches. This was not our own idea, but the Holy Spirit taught me to be aware of their contribution to our church and be thankful for it. With prayer, we have selected several rural churches and have supported them over the years with practical help such as renovation, expansion, and repair of the church buildings either through financial support or by sending Work and Witness teams. We also support those churches that are not self-supporting with their monthly rent and salary for pastors who are starting churches either directly or indirectly.

We do not stop looking for things for which to give thanks to the Lord. As a church, we will keep praying with one heart clearly and precisely, and we will continue to find new ministries that can be started right away.

39 ⊕ REBUILD THE COLLAPSED TEMPLE

On Jeju Island there is a mysterious road. When you stop your car in the middle of the hill with your gear in neutral and your foot off the brake, you will be surprised to see your car going smoothly up the hill by itself rather than sliding down. I myself experienced this phenomenon and was amazed. I even poured water on the hill to confirm that even the water went upstream. People call this place Mysterious Road or Ghost Road. More surprising, however, is that the geological survey of the area finds that, even though the road looks like it is ascending, it is actually lower than its surroundings, and vice versa.

Likewise, everything we see with our eyes is not always truth. There are wide paths that look good in our eyes and seem to lead to success. But to know whether it really is the path of success, we need to reflect biblically. The path the Bible says to be true is the very path leading us to success. Although, in our eyes, the road sometimes appears to be descending, this is the path we should follow.

With this principle, our church started to help small churches. Because the cost is a financial sacrifice, it seems to be a descending road at first. But I believe this is the very way for both us and them to survive and that it is truly an ascending road. Our church, with a burden of debt to pay, planned how to take steps to help the churches in rural areas. One of the plans was to repair and renovate church buildings. With some research we found churches that needed repairs either due to their age or from natural disasters like typhoons.

The first time we selected which churches to help, our first priority was Nazarene churches. But it was not easy to select reasonably within these parameters. After some time, we decided to be free from criteria. We would just support various churches upon their request on a first-come, first-served basis. Those who are looking for help now are likely the ones who are really needy.

Since this ministry began in 2005, approximately twelve individual churches have been supported. Building-repair ministry is special in that we provide labor by sending our people as Work & Witness teams, along with the budget for building materials. It is usually done during summer vacation so church members can easily find time to volunteer. I always see Work & Witness team members feeling proud of fulfilling such a meaningful job during this hot season. If we are not able to fully support a church for their building project, we still try to find significant ways to help.

Our church should continue to grow and do ministry alongside these sister churches. By our words, and also by our practical sharing, we can live as true sisters. I wish to present greater hope to pastors in rural areas who are praying and shedding tears to save souls where they are. I believe this is a way our church will ascend the hill together with them. Some still might be convinced this is not an ascending but a descending road that gives us some disadvantage. Others would argue that we could focus more on the ministries inside the church and be more fruitful. But I am sure it is an ascending road in the eyes of the Lord. I pray that our church will be continually used for this precious ministry.

40 ⊕ RECALLING THE DAYS

Oprah Winfrey is known as one of the most influential American television personalities. Her talk shows aired in more than 132 countries, with an audience of more than 15 million viewers. It is well known that she did not have an easy childhood. Born to a single mother in 1954, she grew up tossed and torn between her grandmother, her mother, and her father. Yet she confesses she overcame all the sorrow and pain through the Word of God. The quote "Having more than others is not a blessing but a mission" has been attributed to her. It suggests that whether we have fortune, health, knowledge, or whatever we have been given, we need to use these gifts for others because they are our mission. Another statement credited to Oprah Winfrey is, "Having more pain than others is not suffering but a calling."

Oprah invited to appear on her talk show a woman who used drugs as a way of forgetting her painful memories of being raped. As the woman shared her trauma, Oprah admitted her own experience of being sexually abused as a child. Oprah's confession moved the heart of her guest and helped bring restoration to her life.

It is never easy to empathize with others, especially those in painful situations. But when we have had a similar experience, we can understand their heart. Ministers also experience various difficulties. Sometimes we encounter fellow ministers who have had similar types of pain. We can then empathize with each other more than others could. And in the midst, we are strongly assured of the work God has done to lead us out of these trials. This is also true of church members who share the same experiences of pain in the church. These church members will find the empathy of others who have been placed in similar situations.

Our church once worshiped in a rented space. We had some financial difficulties as well as various obligations to fulfill as the tenant. By the grace of God, we are now in our own building, but we will never forget the old days. In my country there are still a number of churches worshiping in rented spaces. We would like to present some hope to them because we understand their difficulties. God may directly change their environment, or sometimes he uses other hands to do the mission. If he allows us, we would like to be the mediator to give them gifts. This is the perfect opportunity for us to return the blessings from God to God's church.

During the days of our rented church, I experienced the abundant grace of God many times. Truly, I was not ready to be a full-time pastor in church ministry. Although I had committed myself to the ministry, my main assignment was to teach in the seminary, so I was aware I was not quite equipped for church ministry. I learned there is a great difference between these two areas of ministry, and I had to relearn my ministerial resources. Additionally, I was burdened that the church was worshiping in a rented space and not our own sanctuary. But God poured out his grace on me and led me to pursue this ministry. God has granted his wisdom to me in every moment. With his help, our church was not only able to worship in our own sanctuary, but we were also able to help other churches.

My wish is that my sharing will present a string of hope to all ministers who face real difficulties and are discouraged or in despair. Here is my encouragement to them: *You can do it. I, who never prepared to be a church pastor, was also able to get through it. More than that, you can do everything when God is with you!* I hope that I can always empathize with pastors having difficulties and also with people who are exposed to many problems. I know that kind of heart is a great treasure in working together.

41 ⊕ A CHURCH RAISING UP ANOTHER CHURCH

The apostle Paul said, "I know what it is to be in need, and I know what it is to have plenty. I have learned the secret of being content in any and every situation, whether well fed or hungry, whether living in plenty or in want" (Philippians 4:12). The attitude of a heart of contentment works like a thermostat. Yet people now often live as thermometers and not thermostats. The indicator of the thermometer moves up and down according to its environment. When the weather gets warmer, the mercurial column automatically goes up, and the cold weather brings it down. The thermometer indicates changes according to the exterior environment, but it never changes the temperature itself. The thermostat works differently. It automatically works to increase the temperature when the weather gets colder. Likewise, it also works to decrease the temperature when it gets warmer. In that sense, the contented heart is not like the thermometer that is changed by the environment but, rather, like the thermostat that overcomes the environment.

God has endowed us with the same ability as that of a thermostat. We are not to be controlled by our environment. People in whom the Holy Spirit dwells and the church in which the Holy Spirit stays will never yield to the conditions of the environment. Rather, those infused with the Holy Spirit change the conditions of the environments around themselves. This disposition will not only change our own problems, but it will also help others to understand and overcome their difficulties, just like what a thermostat does.

Our church has been faithful to help poor churches renovate their old sanctuaries and also support rented churches. Sometimes we encounter desperate churches that call for a bigger commitment. Those we approach with more sacrifice. We give them our whole help, not just partial help. With this commitment we started to fully support pastors to plant new churches. In 2004, one of the general superintendents in our denomination visited us. I promised him we would plant three churches in the coming years. We also gave him our word to grow our own church to more than 1,500 memberships. Thankfully, we have about 1,300 people attending the Sunday worship service. In our church, every member is required to attend the Sunday service. If they fail to attend over more than six months, they are automatically taken out of their church responsibilities. So our membership of 1,300 means the number of those who regularly attend the Sunday worship service.

Our commitment was not due to our promise to one person. Neither did the general superintendent push us to do it. I believe it is by the grace of God that we could even give this pledge to him. Our church-planting ministry was possible through a God-given commitment along with our personal promise, all blended for the mission.

As part of our commitment, we reconstructed sanctuaries in three churches, and we dedicated them to the Lord. In one church we demolished the old sanctuary and built a new one. In another we repaired and renovated a sanctuary that collapsed during a typhoon. And for the other we constructed a parsonage, church offices, and a restroom for a new addition.

During this mission, we were deeply touched by the responses of the recipients. The first church was built at the request of the senior pastor, and we just helped them with what they wanted—to build their own church building. I cannot forget what the senior pastor told me: "I still feel like I am dreaming. Sometimes I am confused whether it is still my vision or a reality. We do appreciate Sangamdong Church, who fully donated for this building. We also commit ourselves to the mission of the Lord. We even decided to rename our church and took the old name of Sangamdong Church, which is Sungam church."

It feels shameful for us to receive that kind of appreciation because we are merely paying the debt of love from God. We were very blessed by their appreciation.

This ministry had special meaning as we celebrated the hundredth anniversary of the Church of the Nazarene, as well as the sixtieth anniversary of the Korean Church of the Nazarene. We are still praying to continue this ministry, and we pray the Lord will open various opportunities. I also pray that Sangamdong Church will be used for the glorious ministries of God and become a continuous debt payer to him.

42 ⊕ THE BUDGET: NEVER TO BE GRUDGED OR SPARED

God commanded us, "You shall have no other gods before me" (Exodus 20:3). It is known that in some cultures, there exist hundreds of gods. The Bible clearly tells us those are idols. But people who do not know of God keep creating gods in their life that can pacify their anxieties.

So do any Christians have idols in their lives? Can we say that we only worship our Lord Jehovah? Probably not. A lot of times, money or power becomes an idol. Initially, people seek to possess resources for their basic needs, yet later they believe those things can bring happiness and security to their lives. Soon their possessions become more valuable to them than God is.

"No one can serve two masters. . . . You cannot serve both God and money," said Jesus in Matthew 6:24. Wise people know how to use money in the right way. Those who only know to collect the money are called money keepers, those who love the money are its servants, and those who worship money are its slaves. Money is just one of the means in our lives and cannot be the purpose itself.

Most of all, we need to understand who owns all of the materials, and that is God. Although we may be able to confess it, it is still difficult to be aware of that fact in our lives. We easily misunderstand that money comes from people, so some people are more afraid of men than of God. For example, some can be more fearful of their boss than the Lord. They may be easily absent from the worship service if it pleases their boss, and they justify their behavior with the excuse of making a living. But the owner of everything is our Lord. We think the salary is given by the boss, but it is ultimately God who allows what is given to us.

On our church board this becomes a critical issue among the members. Operating the church as well as serving the various ministries consumes a great deal of the budget. This budget includes serving the community and supporting other churches with a debtor's heart. Since 2006, we have granted support to forty churches with a monthly allocation of $100,000. For systematic support we once cooperated with an organization called Reviving the Korean Church Movement. It helped us support the churches transparently and systematically. The budget assigned to this ministry was at least 60 percent of our total budget. In one year it even exceeded 62 percent. Yet, during our own church construction, we were able to allocate only 26 percent. Honestly, it was not an easy task to give this 26 percent at that time. We could not cease the ministry because we believed it was a way for us to survive together. And I believe this may bring hope once again to Korean church growth.

As I shared earlier, urban church growth in my country cannot be credited to the ability of the senior pastors of the churches. The more growth the urban churches experience, the less the pastors of the churches should enjoy the material blessings. They need to return the blessings to the rural churches with a debtor's heart. They should not grudgingly give back to them. The large, urban churches should not forget that their growth is based on the sacrifice of the rural churches. Supporting these churches will still be our major ministry allocation. Money may come and go. How hard you work to collect it will be erased when God provides a way. If it is God's will for you, money will be given.

One thing ministers should not set aside is acknowledging the sovereignty of the Lord in regard to finances. If shaken, conflicts and frustration rise up among the members. Of course, there are times we are shaken even when we confess the sovereignty of the Lord. Some might be tempted to use the budget for our own church, which brings conflict. But I pray even then that we trust in the Lord and confess that he is the owner of what we have. Above all, let us remember that we are obligated to return the debt through our mission. Let us not be proud of or brag about what we contribute to them but act more humbly, as debtors.

43 ⊕ BEING ONE WITH PEOPLE

Pain guarantees a prize. Even with a wounded body, there is still a way to survive. The place where you stumbled is the very place where you will stand up. The most desperate moment may be the most hopeful moment. The morning star shows up in the darkest sky. Hope may be delayed, but it always prevails.

We underwent difficult situations while actively supporting other Korean churches. There were times that we literally did not see any hope. There were financial problems along with other visible issues, yet the most challenging trial was the lack of harmony among members. I understand it is not guaranteed that every member will be fully supportive of helping other churches while we also need help. It is natural for church members to serve the ministries the church is involved in, yet they might be burdened if the requirement is heavy.

Thankfully, a majority of our church members supported our special ministry, but I could still hear negative voices. Some grumbled that it was excessive while others argued for our church to earn its reputation through this ministry. I thought this was a critical issue that might even cease our mission toward our national church. But I could not raise my voice only; I also had to respect the other opinions. It was frustrating for me to accept those criticisms while I deeply desired to pursue the ministry and encourage them to cooperate.

Then God intervened and helped me overcome this crisis. In the midst of my struggle, he strengthened me through his words, and I could stand on the biblical truth. The Word of God is available to give all Christians wisdom. When the minister approaches his ministry with a firm biblical foundation, there is no reason for people not to follow and joyfully help. To help my own congregation understand, I went back to the basics and focused on teaching the Word of God to our people. The Bible clearly teaches us to give a helping hand to the needy. It does not teach us to fill our own stomachs and pockets with the resources we are given.

"There will always be poor people in the land. Therefore, I command you to be openhanded toward your fellow Israelites who are poor and needy in your land" (Deuteronomy 15:11).

"Give, and it will be given to you. A good measure, pressed down, shaken together and running over, will be poured into your lap. For with the measure you use, it will be measured to you" (Luke 6:38).

As I gained spiritual food through the Bible, I was strengthened. Any objections or resistance became powerless before the word of the Lord. After this divine intervention, I always sought the Word of God, not depending on debates anymore. Even in this process, I needed to be wise. Simply presenting the Scriptures and arguing that I was right and they were wrong would've made things even worse. We all needed to learn and understand the biblical truths. Statements like, "We need to do this because this is what God wants" or, "Just obey the Word of God" are not suitable. The Bible itself has the absolute authority, yet we do not want to be domineering over others with its truth. A minister has a duty to awaken his or her people to their call and mission.

I am thankful to the Lord, who sustained me during those crises. I am also grateful to our people, who have been so supportive in every ministry. I believe we can be even more unified now because of those days when we struggled. Hope and dreams are the wings of our spirit. If we have hope for tomorrow, today's despair is not a problem. The most wretched thought is not failing to achieve our hopes and dreams but, rather, being without any hopes or dreams. Our church has clear hopes and dreams. The problems and issues we face are not of consequence to us. If God blesses those hopes and dreams, we will surely overcome whatever obstacles we face.

44 ⊕ A SENDING CHURCH

Greg Mortenson wrote a book called *Three Cups of Tea*. In it, Mortenson described how he climbed the mountain K2 in Pakistan in memory of his deceased sister. During his ascent he and other climbers met a hiker in danger, and they rescued him. On the way down, the author lost his way and arrived alone in a small village in the Himalayas, and he was cared for by the villagers.

Mortenson wanted to pay back their kindness to him. Their lives were happy, but there was one thing they hoped for—a school to educate their children. After he returned to the United States, Mortenson worked hard to raise funds to help them. It was certainly a challenge to build a school in that remote mountainous area. He received death threats from Islamic clerics who were against educating girls. He was also the recipient of hate mail from Americans who were opposed to helping Muslim children. In spite of the obstacles, Mortenson never gave up raising funds for his mission. He eventually helped build seventy-eight schools in Himalayan villages without roads. His efforts provided schools for more than thirty thousand children. This is not just a story that touches our hearts, but is a miracle to the people whose lives it changed. And this miracle did not happen in just one day but through the sweat of a committed person.

Mortenson's story helps inspire Christians to a passion for foreign missions. Our church has attempted to maintain a balance between foreign and domestic missions. Our church seldom goes out of the country for mission trips, but we do our part to support career and long-term missionaries. Supporting missional institutions is one of our strategies. We have supported a missionary family who teach and serve as faculty at Asia-Pacific Nazarene Theological Seminary. We have also been able to give regularly to the global Church of the Nazarene through the Asia-Pacific regional office based in Singapore. We have sent long-term missionaries abroad, and now we dream of networking with various missionaries.

In 3 John 1:5–8, the author is writing to those who welcomed and cared for people sent out as strangers to share the gospel. He is pleased with their good deeds. They did not go to the field for direct evangelism but took a role of welcoming and caring for evangelists. The scripture mentions that both of them "work together for the truth" (v. 8).

Sending missionaries is also an important mission. We can participate in missions by sending and supporting those who will evangelize without actually going to the field ourselves. Yet sometimes we see people who are not serious in sending missionaries. Some do not value the small amount of financial support or prayer support, but those things are critical when we send missionaries. The support may seem little to individual donors, but it is significant when multiplied with others. It may not appear substantial to some but can turn out to be a great deal of support to missionaries in the field. Imagine there is a man who was not able to drink a sip of water for a whole day. A cup of water would be a great supply to that man. Generally a cup of water might be regarded as unworthy, but it could be a critical help in some situations. Likewise, small resources and prayer could be desperately needed at just the right time and in just the right place.

Our church was never involved in building churches overseas but was more focused on sending missionaries to fulfill their call. We teach our church members to give and sacrifice even in small amounts. We emphasize how valuable and beautiful it is in the eyes of the Lord. We will keep finding creative ways to support foreign missions in the coming years. We will send as many missionaries as God allows. We will be missional by being a sending church of as many missionaries as we can. In whatever ways you find, I hope every church will make foreign evangelism a priority.

45 ⊕ OVERCOMING LIMITATIONS

There was a famous sports commentator who had a rich knowledge of and prestigious career in the game of baseball. He became a coach of a professional baseball team. Yet his team had a miserable record of fifteen wins and forty losses. He was terminated as the coach and returned to his seat as a commentator. He later said, "I will never go back to the field." There are great differences between being a commentator of the game and being a good coach who can lead a team to victory.

For a sports game, we need a good commentator, but we also need a good coach. Commentators do not always have firsthand experience with games, but they help their audience have a better understanding, and they make watching the games more enjoyable. Meanwhile, we also need the coach who will train the team to win games, although they are not able to provide exciting comments on the games to the public. In addition to the commentator and coach, there are various other roles in the game of baseball. Players have different roles as well, according to the positions they play. This principle doesn't only apply to the sport of baseball but also to organizations. There are various positions and roles to play, and each one carries out a given task. When everyone does their best where they are situated, the whole body functions well.

Nothing about this is different in church ministry. It is even truer in foreign missions. An individual cannot take on all the roles alone. We should not become discouraged when we find it difficult to carry out a certain area of ministry. We should not feel overloaded or burdened to fulfill the mission by any means, being reminded there are others who can carry those loads. Our job is to give the best efforts to our own area, helping and cooperating with others within that circle.

For this reason, Sangamdong Church values the network of missions. We do our best in our own position yet try to build up a good network to work together. When we find our own limitations, we can easily ask for help within the network and be ready to provide prompt hands to others when needed.

In most cases, Korean churches who send their missionaries overseas also feel obligated to support all the financial needs, including living expenses. However, things can change. A church may no longer be able to fully support its missionaries, or a missionary may leave the mission field. In either case, the mission field will be seriously disadvantaged. It is not always easy for the sending church to communicate closely with the missionaries in the field and support them according to their immediate needs.

Because of a concern for these potential problems, our church wanted to be involved in the network for missions. This network could look for and provide other resources to the ministry even if the missionaries had to leave the field suddenly. It is also helpful when we start a new foreign mission. For example, if our church starts a new mission in Thailand, we cannot hit the ground running on our own. But the situation changes when we can communicate and cooperate with the missionaries already within the network in Thailand. The ministry will be even more efficient due to their knowledge of and experience in Thailand. It is also easier to build trust within the network.

Our church dispatched a missionary family several years ago. They served as professors at Asia-Pacific Nazarene Theological Seminary, which is accredited by the local educational board. Because we already had an existing network, we were able to send the missionary family to this school, one of the few Protestant seminaries accredited by the Philippine government. When we send missionaries with the proper knowledge and understanding about the mission field, connected within the network, we can carry out our mission more effectively based on the higher level of established trust. Our church will continue to be committed to working with the hands already in the strong and active network of God.

46 ⊕ SPONSORING SEMINARIANS

On October 20, 1968, the marathon was the final highlight of the Mexico Olympics. John Stephen Akhwari, a Tanzanian runner, along with numerous other marathoners, was faithfully running the race. In the middle of the course, however, he fell down and sustained a serious injury to his knee. Insisting that he continue, he returned to the race after simple emergency care. With a bloody bandage on his knee, he did not stop running. The winner had already completed the race an hour earlier. But some in the audience still waited for Akhwari, who was running injured with all of his strength. Sirens and whistles of police officers were heard from the marathon gate. Akhwari entered the stadium to run the final lap of the race, still limping. He never stopped or gave up, even in the midst of his injury and pain. The audience stood to cheer and honor him until he crossed the finish line. When he was interviewed later and asked why he did not give up and how he could complete the race in such pain, he answered, "My country did not send me ten thousand miles just to start the race. They sent me to finish the race."

A Christian's life is driven by mission. We will be called by God to heaven when our mission on this earth is complete. To the Tanzanian runner, winning the title was not his ultimate goal. His goal was to complete the race to honor the country that had sent him ten thousand miles to represent them. It is an important fact to remember as a church. The fact that an individual can set a clear goal does not always come by self-motivation. For Akhwari, his country and their support motivated him. If he had not been running the Olympic race but a local marathon instead, for his own personal achievement, a serious injury like the one he sustained might have caused him to give up and not finish.

This concept can also apply to students. Although most students are able to set their goals and run toward them on their own, there are times that challenge their sustainability. Some do not have a clear vision in setting their goals. They work hard but do not know exactly where to target—even in seminary. Students come to seminary believing they are called by God and given a divine mission. Yet they might not have clear goals set for the future. The church has a mission for them, though. Just as Tanzania was a strong supporter of their runner, the church should be the strong supporter of young seminarians.

Sangamdong Church has been praying for this mission. We desire to support more students in our Nazarene educational institutions who are within our network. I believe these students will develop a strong sense of mission and duty more than ever before through our sponsoring. Along with their sense of responsibility to complete academic courses, it will enable them to set clear visions. Of course, it might take some time for them to have a clear direction for mission. But they will not be discouraged by a lack of support, and they will be able to focus on their given task. They will be motivated to meet the expectations of the supporters and show them their very best.

Developing human capabilities is a very important mission in our church. Both internationally and nationally, we hope to raise up people and academic institutions.

I believe the hope of our country is in the church. God will be pleased with our country when our churches are strong. The righteous churches should stand up. Righteous pastors are necessary to lead them. Raising up the right people is, therefore, essential.

Our hope is not fully realized yet. But I am humbly jotting down my wish list with a string of hope that it will come true one day. I fervently pray the churches will be able to faithfully support future ministers so more will be called each year and give their lives for the glory of God's kingdom in numerous places.

47 ⊕ WISHES FOR THE FUTURE PASTOR

There was a boy who lost his dad at the age of thirteen. He then lost his eyesight in a sporting accident the very next year. His mother died from a heart attack at the shock of all this tragedy, so his older sister dropped out of high school to care for him. She died within sixteen months of dropping out of school. The boy suddenly became an orphan full of despair and hopelessness.

However, he overcame all obstacles and became a symbol for those with disabilities. This boy was the late Dr. Young Woo Kang, former policy advisor for the National Council on Disability, who served at the White House under U.S. President George W. Bush. He donated $250,000 to the Rotary Club International. When he was diagnosed with pancreatic cancer he confessed, "I can now pay the debt to the love of Christ that holds my hands 'til today." He shared the secret that had changed a hopeless life to a hope-filled life. Dr. Kang stated, "I tried to find a role model who had a similar situation to mine. I told myself, *I can do it if he can* and made myself try to be like him." Dr. Kang eventually made it and became a role model who provided hope and challenge for many with disabilities who previously did not have hope.

Am I finding a role model in my ministry? Am I also a good role model to others? Whenever I think about a role model, I think of Bible college and seminary students at KNU. I have to ask myself if I am a good role model for my congregation at Sangamdong Church of the Nazarene. I have the same burden toward Bible college and seminary students and feel a great need to be a good role model for them, to lead them into Christlikeness and provide essential wisdom in ministry.

When it comes to Bible college and seminary students at KNU, I emphasize ready-made preparation. When they go into ministry right after graduation, they should be ready-made to lead any ministry assignment. Ready-made is to be trained to be ready in advance, and I feel this is important. I also emphasize the Word of the Lord. In class and outside class, I encourage them to read the Bible as the basis for ministerial preparation. I also encourage them to memorize as many verses as possible.

Sadly, many pastors do not have a thorough Bible knowledge, even if they spent many years attending Bible college and seminary. It shows that they are not ready-made for ministry. It may be important to study various academic and theological areas, but a thorough understanding of the Scriptures is imperative. Partial understanding does not help; pastors should understand all of Scripture for various ministry applications.

I am seriously considering implementing a Scripture memorization test of fifty verses in each semester, together with mid-year and final-year exams in the seminary. Students will be rewarded for memorizing three hundred verses in three years of study. I would rather educate pastors who can memorize five hundred verses, as opposed to those who only have better grades with their thesis.

Students wonder why I emphasize memory verses so much. I believe the verses memorized will be treasures for their future ministry. When you preach, you should be able to demonstrate relevant Scripture as proof. The verses in their mouths will become diamonds, not only in the public but also for counseling, prayer, and evangelism.

I often confuse the verses I've memorized. As I grow older, I forget some scriptures. I can memorize in my office but am not sure if I can cite them anymore in the pulpit. So we have to memorize thoroughly. I do not only instruct my students to memorize verses; I also continue to practice memory verses in my own life. When I spend more time memorizing, I can remember them for a longer period of time.

We remember our calling with Scripture verses we have memorized. Our commitment will be strengthened. The Word of God is life, so the memory verses are not just a matter of storing knowledge. When we memorize verses diligently and use them wisely in various situations, they provide us abundant life. The life in us will be transferred to those we meet in our daily lives. I hope to be a good role model to Bible college and seminary students at KNU. Later, they will hopefully be good role models to their congregations. Furthermore, I hope and pray that all Christians are memorizing words that will help them stand with a firm foundation.

48 ⊕ DREAMING FOR ONE MORE RIGHTEOUS MAN

God had a meaningful conversation with Abraham before destroying Sodom and Gomorrah. Abraham asked, "'What if there are fifty righteous people in the city? Will you really sweep it away and not spare the place for the sake of the fifty righteous people in it?'

"The LORD said, 'If I find fifty righteous people in the city of Sodom, I will spare the whole place for their sake.'

"Then Abraham spoke up again: . . . 'What if the number of the righteous is five less than fifty? Will you destroy the whole city for lack of five people?'

"'If I find forty-five there,' he said, 'I will not destroy it'" (Genesis 18:24, 26–28).

In this manner, Abraham reduced the number of righteous men until it came down to ten. God promised, "for the sake of ten" that he would not destroy the city (v. 32). But Sodom and Gomorrah were destroyed because there were not even ten righteous men to be found.

The major causes of the destruction of Sodom and Gomorrah were unrighteousness and sin. But God did not ask the degree of unrighteousness or sin. He only asked the number of righteous men in the city.

I often hear worries for the future and destiny of Korea. Why, then, are we not destroyed? It is because we still have righteous prayer warriors in the country. We need to give our efforts to raise more righteous men and women. I want to see more righteous men and women coming from KNU, and I pray that every single student would become a righteous man or woman.

Of course, we all live in difficult situations, and KNU is no exception. I believe other universities have similar challenges to the ones we face. KNU already has a lower number of new students since 2013. The rate of applying students decreases every year. But crisis does not hinder the life of a righteous man or woman. The righteous will not fade away because of crisis. When we see crisis with earthly perspectives and human hearts, worries come. But we can grow spiritually with these challenges. In this crisis, I am sure that KNU will be reborn into a school that will educate godly and righteous men and women. This, I believe, is my mission, and I will do my best to train more righteous men and women.

KNU has a unique calling because we have the most disabled students in Korea. There are 349 colleges and universities and 6,000 disabled students currently studying in Korea. Among the 6,000 students, 376 of them attend KNU. Among the 376 disabled students, more than 80 percent are severely disabled. KNU specializes in this area. Because we have so many students who are disabled, we have more opportunities to give them a home. I am certain that our KNU students can be raised as righteous in order to save more souls. The graduates will be working not only to overcome their own disabilities but also to save their neighbors, communities, and the nation. This hope pushes me even though we do not seem to have much hope in sight.

A missional heart has the authority to give power to take a risk instead of making us tired and giving up. This heart gives us gratitude for the challenge. If we place our hope in reality, we will fail, but we can give thanks to God if we see the future through his eyes.

There are three kinds of thankfulness. First is *if* thankfulness. *God, if you solve this problem, I **will be** thankful.* This kind of thankfulness is conditional.

Second is *because of* thankfulness. When we look at our past, we have so much to be thankful for. *God, I thank you **because** you allow my child to attend a good college.* This is our thankfulness because of what we have already received.

Third is *in spite of* thankfulness. *I thank the Lord **in spite of** bankruptcy in my business, failing my college entrance exam, and losing my health.*

I hope my thankfulness does not cease in spite of troubles at my university. When we run the race with an attitude of thankfulness despite difficult circumstances, our countries and churches will fill with righteous men and women to help save the world.

49 ⊕ MY WISH FOR KOREAN CHURCHES

I want to share the story of a Korean movie called *Mama*, which was directed by Ikhwan Choi in 2011. The mother in the movie delivers dairy drinks to take care of her son, who suffers from Duchenne Muscular Dystrophy and has been given five years to live. One day she felt ill in the middle of her deliveries. She saw the doctor, who diagnosed her with ovarian cancer and told her she only had a three-month life expectancy. Her cry was to live at least five years with her son. Yet, facing the reality, she felt that her best choice was to die with her son. She planned to give her son a large dose of sleeping pills, telling him they were vitamins. She suggested they play a word game while they waited for his death. She shed continuous tears waiting for her son to fall into eternal sleep. The son, leaning on his mother's back, whispered, "I like the word *hope*. So I put these words on my wall. 'Hope never abandons you—only you abandon hope.'" When the mother heard these words from her son, she changed her mind.

Do we really have a hope? The answer is simple. Everyone has a hope. Yet we cannot grasp the hope that is right in front of us. In the movie, the son held onto hope in the middle of nothing. And he passed the hope on to his mother.

We Christians have the strongest hope because of Jesus Christ. Jesus is the hope for all of our lives. A famous Korean poet, No-hae Park, sings, "Humans are the only hope." Christians should sing, "Jesus is the only hope." And, because of the hope Christ gives us, Korean churches also have hope. Many people have warned that the future of Korean churches is at stake, saying there will be no church growth. But those are only human thoughts. Jesus will not abandon his church. As long as we hold onto Jesus, we have hope in him.

Sangamdong Church of the Nazarene has experienced hope, and I want to share it with others. The stories in this book are full of hope, and I wish to share that hope with Korean churches. Korean churches should follow the image of Christ. Through our various ministries, we have to learn the real, servant leadership of Christ. One of the characteristics of the leadership of Jesus is to *go and find*. Human leaders and kings send their subordinates to go out and find people for them. Yet Jesus himself was the one to go and find people to minister to. He specifically went out to find the sick, women, and children—the underprivileged in the society in which he lived.

Go and find is a way of welcoming, which is to greet someone as they come in. The welcoming of Jesus was beyond our common sense. Jesus welcomed people not by waiting for them to come in but going to welcome them. It is the highest form of welcoming that Jesus demonstrated. The astonishing welcome of Jesus was when he welcomed sinners wholeheartedly. Jesus went and found outcasts. Jesus went and found one after another. He shared meals and fellowship with them. This act was indeed a subject of criticism among the religious leaders of the time.

We teach following the leadership that Christ demonstrated to *go and find* people in need of the gospel. This action should be extended to those who are called sinners in our eyes. I hope and pray that all Korean churches will *go and find* people who are in need, and welcome them. Sangamdong Church of the Nazarene will continue to work hard to follow Christ's model of leadership. We will pray more about where we *go and find*. I pray with my whole heart for all Christians to spread the strong fragrance of Jesus.

50 ⊕ MY WISH FOR KOREAN CHURCHES (PART TWO)

There is an adage called Pareto's Principle that 20 percent of people create 80 percent of results. For instance, in department stores, 80 percent of sales are generated by 20 percent of customers. This principle was asserted by Italian economist Vilfredo Pareto when he studied in England during the nineteenth century. He found that a small number of people create large portions of the national economy. This principle now applies to analyze the current society and church. In other words, in a company or in the church, only 20 percent of the people work hard and actively participate in various functions. Only 20 percent of the power can be a usable source to mobilize the church community.

Do I belong to the 80 percent or the 20 percent? Does my church belong to the 80 percent or the 20 percent in God's kingdom? There is a great example of the 80/20 principle in our early Christian community. The history of the early Christian churches began after the resurrection of Jesus Christ. The strong work of the Holy Spirit began among the disciples in the upper room on the day of Pentecost. The disciples then spread out to tell of the death and resurrection of Jesus Christ. Their efforts formed early Christian communities that were then expanded by the apostle Paul and his followers.

The Romans at that time were the major target group among the disciples. Rome was a hierarchical society, and the Romans accepted the class system, obeying their king as god. In this context, the disciples had to break down the walls of hierarchy. In order to teach the heart of Christ, breaking down cultural barriers was the first job. It was not an easy task. It looked like a revolution that shakes the foundation of a society. But the disciples began to shake the cultural and class structure that was deeply rooted in Roman society. What the disciples emphasized was brotherhood and sisterhood in Christ. They preached equality in Christ because we are all brothers and sisters in Christ.

When we accept Christ as our personal Savior, there is no class division, no slave versus master, no man versus woman. At least, that is what happened in the Christian community. For Korean churches, if we want to learn the true meaning of servant leadership, we have to break class divisions within our society. Serving marginalized people temporarily, or inviting them to church for a special event, is far from adopting a genuine servant heart. Like what the early forefathers did, we have to break the walls of hierarchy. True disciples play a vital role in breaking the church hierarchy and the class biases in society. If we cannot change them, we must at least tell them that the hierarchy is meaningless in Christ. This is the assignment for servant leadership. Without breaking this cultural bias, we cannot genuinely practice true servanthood that comforts the hardships of the marginalized. When churches take on the true meaning of servanthood in Christ, nonbelievers can realize the love of the servant heart of Christians.

The concept of communication is deeply related in fellowship. But the early Christians' communication went beyond just making friendships. For them, genuine fellowship was to share their lives. They even sold their possessions to meet the needs of members in their community. This sacrificial relationship should be practiced not only in the church community but also in the world. Jesus did not teach us that the early Christian church was for pleasure in fellowship among ourselves. Sacrifice is a love based on the giving up of myself to fill the needs of others. This spirit is the leadership of the church toward the world.

The world is changed by small numbers of people. Like the early Christian churches, Korean churches should be that small number to change the world. If we overcome class division to share the love of God, making communication and equal relationships, the days will surely come.

⊕ EPILOGUE

Sangamdong Church of the Nazarene was planted soon after the Korean War by the Alabaster offerings of the International Church of the Nazarene in June 1955. By the grace of God, I was installed as the senior pastor at the forty-fifth anniversary celebration in June 2000. I began my first, full-time pastoral ministry at this church. I thought it was an honor to be the pastor of Sangamdong Church of the Nazarene, and God blessed me so much by growing the church more than twenty times over a period of ten years.

The key to this rapid church growth was the *ministry makeover.* In 2003, the congregation planned for a new church building. I prayed the new building would create a strong social presence for the local communities. The makeover began in me, to make myself a responsible pastor to the congregation. When I was a Bible college student, I did not faithfully attend the dawn prayer meeting because I did not consider it important in my spiritual life. But as a pastor, I had to lead and preach at the dawn prayer meeting every day. I did not go home after the prayer meeting but stayed at my office until 10:00 p.m. each evening. The dawn prayer meeting attendance was not increasing, but I did not give up. I asked my church members to give me their family pictures in order that I could pray for each of them. I prayed for one after another by calling their names out to the Lord. Gradually, the attendance of the prayer meeting increased as church attendance also grew. In order to transform the church, I had to transform myself first. I had to be an example and present a good image of a pastor to my congregation.

And I continued to make efforts to present a good image of our church to our local communities. To be salt and light is a commandment of Jesus Christ (Matthew 5:13–14). I focused on compassionate ministry toward marginalized people in the communities. My emphasis on the ministry makeover was echoed in the blueprint of the new church building. When construction began, there were not many amenities that provided services to the communities near the church. I wanted to provide community-friendly facilities. I planned a daycare center on the first floor. The sanctuary and pastoral offices were on the second floor. On the third floor would be Silver School, the weekly program for senior citizens, and a speech therapy center would be on the fourth floor.

This was not an easy idea. It was impossible to receive a building permit for a daycare center in the church. The city planning did not permit the operation of a daycare in the current location. Yet God miraculously orchestrated an open door that led to starting a daycare center. Sangamdong Church of the Nazarene gradually spread the sweet fragrance of Jesus and became an integral part of the community. Socially marginalized people received firsthand benefits from our church's ministry.

The ministry makeover was not only for the local congregation and communities. The construction of a Christlike image went beyond our walls and reached out to other churches in need. Of course, churches *should* have a servant heart and share the love of God. Other churches also need to be recipients of Christlike love and care. I do not forget all that Sangamdong Church of the Nazarene once received from the Lord, and I wanted to share those blessings with other churches in need. We can't but help those churches that are in a similar situation to our past. Sangamdong Church was able to provide financial support and a remodel of an old sanctuary. We also extended our financial support toward rural churches. The more financial support the church gives for helping other churches in need, the more blessings we receive from the Lord, and it is our responsibility to share the blessings from the Lord. In fact, it is our duty as disciples. We also participated in overseas ministries by partnering with Nazarene Missions to support missionaries and a seminary in the Asia-Pacific region.

Through the emphasis of the ministry makeover, Sangamdong Church served the local communities. What I would like to emphasize at this point is that servanthood should be the objective and not the means. The motive for serving the communities should not be to increase church membership. We do not abuse the ministry makeover for the purpose of church growth. We want local communities to use our church as much as they need, by sending their children to the daycare center, their senior citizens to Silver School, and those with speech disabilities to the speech therapy center. Of course, I would be happy to see an increase in church membership as a direct fruit of these ministries. Yet true servanthood does not allow us to pursue the ministry makeover as a means to church growth. Statistically, 60 to 70 senior citizens regularly attend Silver School. Yet Sangamdong Church did not gain a single member from the outreach for a long time. If our goal was to increase membership of the church, the Silver School operation was not a productive or profitable ministry in terms of cost. The speech therapy center was a similar example.

Many churches have tried to offer community-oriented services with the purpose of church growth in mind. I do not mean to *oppose* church growth by providing community services. But the heart of servanthood focuses on how best to serve the community, not for the purpose of church growth. Evangelism should be the multiplication of God's communities and not my own local church growth.

Sadly, non-Christians look suspiciously at church-based, community outreach for increasing membership of the church. Some people do not welcome church-based, community outreach programs. Sangamdong Church now receives so much trust from the local community because they know that our community services are based on true servanthood as the goal and not the means. We will continue to do our best to save lost souls, but our ministry focus is to lead them to become children of God by prayer and support. We see the fruit of our efforts in ministry. We see people knocking at our church doors to become part of the church. They often have been referred by the local community center, who recommended our church by saying we are trustworthy and good. Isn't this the true meaning of ministry makeover?

A church should serve communities after a model of the life and ministry of Jesus Christ. But we have to be careful of the two traps of pride and boastfulness. The more we spend time in successful ministries, the more we begin to feel proud of ourselves and boastful. In order to prevent these attempts by Satan, we have to keep one thing in mind, and that is to have the heart of a debtor.

We never forget our heart as a debtor. We do not want to forget the fact that the enormous growth of Sangamdong Church in Seoul is not the result of our excellence but because of the sacrificial ministry and discipleship of rural churches. Due to the urbanization process of a few decades, many Christians have migrated from various provinces and begun attending Sangamdong Church. Therefore, we should not be boastful or feel proud for helping rural churches. We should be ashamed for not extending more support.

The debtor's heart longs to serve local communities. We have received God's grace, and we are mindful of those who do not know him. It is as if you are in a wrecked ship in the ocean and are rescued by a boat. Can you allow your eyes to avoid those who are not yet saved? We will give our best to reach out to people who are drowning in the ocean. Our souls have been saved, and we feel indebtedness to the Lord. The rescue mission is not something we are boastful of. It is our duty.

Early church forefathers planted churches wherever they went, and the churches became the centers in serving and evangelizing the community members. Today, the responsibility has not changed. Churches should be the root and center of serving and evangelism. This is the sole responsibility of the community church.

Sangamdong Church reminds us of our local responsibility. We feel accountable to lead the community to Christ by serving its people. If all Korean churches felt responsible to be the center of their communities in serving the disregarded people in their areas, the kingdom of God would be expanded. I pray the wave of the love of Christ among contemporary Christians would be the same as that of the early church disciples in spreading the Word of the Lord.

When a church is focused on ministry to the communities *outside* the church, communication *within* the church is imperative. Members of the church will need to understand the importance of the ministry in order to earn the support of the congregation. Even if servanthood to local communities is essential, pastors often achieve the opposite effect if they make their own decisions. Trustworthy pastoral leadership should be established prior to external community outreach.

Leadership should be based on a solid, biblical foundation. If necessary, local churches can use various educational programs. A church can serve its community more powerfully only when the members of the church understand the biblical foundation of servanthood and voluntarily participate in various ministry opportunities.

Sangamdong Church also had many struggles within the congregation to provide various outreach ministries. Gradually we were able to overcome these obstacles by the Word of the Lord.

Do you have a clear vision from the Lord? Do you have a strong mission from the Lord? If so, the vision and mission should be carried out without interruption of human judgment. Do not worry; do not hesitate. Stay firmly tuned to the Word of the Lord. We can participate in God's great ministry by communicating within the congregation in unity and harmony in the Word of the Lord.

I have shared how God has poured out his grace in the midst of my ministry. In the center of his grace is enormous church growth of twenty times within ten years. But that is not all. The ministry makeover is important as the universal answer to church growth. But there are always limitations, and the strategies can change with time and context. If we only stick with one strategy, we may become stubborn, and there will be no room to grow.

If you experience God's grace with a ministry makeover in church growth, you need to depend on the work of the Holy Spirit for greater church revival. Ministry makeovers can misguide the spiritual growth of the congregation if they become routine or habit, and this will hinder church growth. True growth can be possible only when the congregation experiences the powerful work of the Holy Spirit and they pursue excellence in the Spirit. More often than not, we hear that church planting is hard. It is also difficult to make a church grow. But what I learned is that we can do it. I kept notes of what I learned during my ministry. I shared how pastors should lead and the ways lay leaders can participate in order to enable church growth. I also proposed better ways by acknowledging the mistakes I made.

Sangamdong Church of the Nazarene will thrive under new goals. We have healthy church growth by focusing on being a good church that serves the community. From now on, we are setting a higher goal from good church to great church. A good church is not always a powerful church. A powerful church can be achieved through a genuine transformation of the congregation. I am longing to hear people say, "You will be transformed when you go to this church" or have others say, "My friend was radically changed after attending this church."

For Sangamdong Church to become a great church, we need to surrender ourselves and our ministry wholeheartedly to the Holy Spirit. I will continue to pray that the Lord will lead this congregation with his mighty power. If that happens, those hurt and powerless people will be radically transformed by the power of the Spirit, and they will dare to live a holy life. I have a dream that Sangamdong Church of the Nazarene will be one of the models of a great church in Korea.